An Unknown Angel's Gift

A Couple's Lung Transplant Journey

Cherie S. Blackwell

Copyright © 2023 Cherie S. Blackwell
All rights reserved
First Edition

Fulton Books
Meadville, PA

Published by Fulton Books 2023

ISBN 979-8-88731-015-2 (paperback)
ISBN 979-8-89221-068-3 (hardcover)
ISBN 979-8-88731-016-9 (digital)

Printed in the United States of America

I N MEMORY OF MY FATHER, Greg, who we lost unexpectedly in 2020 and who was an unwavering support system during our extensive wait for my husband's lifesaving transplant.

Those we love don't go away; they walk beside us every day.

Contents

Prologue vii

Chapter 1 1
Chapter 2 15
Chapter 3 43
Chapter 4 68
Chapter 5 85
Chapter 6 104
Chapter 7 112
Chapter 8 121
Chapter 9 133
Chapter 10 150
Chapter 11 223
Chapter 12 235
Chapter 13 286
Chapter 14 315
Chapter 15 327

Prologue

Robert sat up in his hospital bed, staring out the window, looking perplexed. I could read his thoughts. He had that "do I deserve this" look. Did I do the right thing? After coming to, after a lengthy transplant surgery, he turned to look at me and said, "Am I okay?" He trusted me with the answer of yes.

When I think of my husband, I think of a hero. Here is someone I watched struggle with a debilitating, exhausting, relentless, endless lung disease for years. In all those years, I never heard any form of negativity or complaints come from his mouth. You think of courage and the many definitive forms it can take on—physical, emotional, and mental. The courage I saw in my husband on this journey made me a better person and is the primary reason I write this book. To watch someone struggle with disease and exert so much courage and strength is an amazing beautiful task. It makes you look at life differently. It makes you appreciate every day and all the things that go with your day-to-day endeavors. You cannot put yourselves in their shoes—only sympathize and be supportive and do your best to show that you are strong when inside you are scared to death of what the future brings. It is a journey where you feel helpless at times, but you become stronger by watching their strength and positive attitude. You learn from them and so many others you come across. What a gift each day is.

I remember meeting my husband twenty years ago; and the strong, mysterious, smart, funny, charismatic charm was electrifying. We developed a friendship—the romantic love you read about. This was a person I could confide in, trust, and fall in love with. Robert had all of these traits and a lung condition, which followed him for years and years. I remember fairly new into our relationship, he needed a second lung surgery (I was not with him for the first). I remember walking into the hospital room to visit, and he looked at me with such gratitude (the same as he had so many years later for yet another). The doctor asked if I wanted to stay with him in the room, and I said yes. I clearly remember earlier that day the doctor telling me, "He has bad lungs," albeit he did wonderfully. I saw a hero that day in bed, and he still is to this day.

There are many things you will discover on this journey: the acceptance, the denial, the adjustments, the truth to what to expect, and the tools to hopefully help anyone who reads this to accept and adjust as we did on a long journey to what turned out to be a new lease on life for both of us.

Chapter 1

Acceptance

Acceptance doesn't mean resignation; it means understanding that something is what it is and that there's got to be a way through it.
—Michael J. Fox

EVEN AS I BEGIN THIS, tears stream down my face. I remember that fateful day at the pulmonologist specialty office. It was eight years ago on a spring day in March. We were not sure what to expect as our primary care doctor referred us to the lung specialist after Robert had nearly collapsed at work, feeling winded. After extensive tests and lengthy exams, he called us into his office, telling us, "There is not enough oxygen supplying your heart with exertion." He prescribed oxygen for Robert in the evenings and with exertion as well as aspirin and heartburn medication; and he recommended pulmonary rehabilitation exercising, more x-rays, and a consult with a heart doctor. I will never forget the hurt, disgusted look on my husband's face when the doctor said he had to be on oxygen. Robert had just been promoted recently at his place of employment and knew being on oxygen would ultimately affect his career. Having an extreme illness is not something you expect to hear at our age in this stage of our lives. Here we were, together for ten years and married for six, enjoying life, our careers, hobbies, vacation, family, and friends. You do not expect to begin this long journey of doctor appointments and a total transition of your schedule and life.

From that day forward, our lives changed forever. We left the office in shock, and I thought, *Please, God, give us strength to get through this because I know it is not going to be a condition we can manage with medicine or oxygen alone or where one visit to a doctor can solve the problem.* I remember getting home and Robert saying, "You can leave if you want to." I replied, "This marriage is for better or for worse. We will get through this." Thus, we proceeded to go on our journey of one-after-another tests and doctor appointments.

These were not simple in-and-out-the-door tests and appointments. They were scheduled around our schedule and the doctors; and there were insurance factors as well, which involved numerous phone calls and time, which I took over to save my husband the added stress. The rest of March involved numerous CTs, x-rays, ultrasounds, and echoes done at the cardiologist office and hospital and numerous IV drugs injected as well as another consult with a physical/pulmonary therapist who, in turn, stated that Robert needed to be seen at a different facility. April and May heart tests revealed no fluid around his heart, hardening of arteries, heart attacks, or congestive heart failure; the water retention was pulmonary related. He was given meds for the water and potassium. The therapist said, "Return to your pulmonologist, as per your cardiologist." The pulmonologist reviewed his chest x-rays and notified us that his CT scan revealed a complete bullous emphysema. Then we discussed a lung transplant in the future and were given a referral to the downtown Henry Ford Transplant Institute in Detroit. Furthermore, this appointment was made in May; however, before we could go to that, Robert came down with pneumonia a week beforehand and was prescribed a heavy dose of antibiotics and Prednisone (the wonder drug for inflammation), and back to the hospital for x-rays and tests. During this weekend, Robert had fever, chills, body aches, and bowel issues. It was like his whole being was in withdrawal from everything. This was the beginning of accepting everything. There was no drinking with work acquaintances or each other. This was appearing more and more serious to us as the days passed.

Before all of this, Robert and I always prided ourselves on enjoying our lives to the fullest, both of us with full-time fulfilling jobs while being able to rollerblade in the park; go out in our muscle car (which is a stick shift); go to hockey games; barbeque; and travel the United States for wonderful vacations to gamble, sightsee, hike, rest and relax, enjoy time with friends, and spoil/see all our nieces and nephews.

So as you journey into acceptance, think about how an illness can impact a young adult in their young, married, vibrant life. There are so many contributing factors. First of all, your schedule completely changes. You adjust it to doctor appointments, and what your normal daily routine was? Well, that changes. In our case, my husband, Robert, worked five to seven days a week, ten hours a day, starting early in the morning. So he'd leave before I got up, and he'd be home before me. I would get up, have a workout routine, and plan for the day with a lot of time to spare—me time, so to speak. Robert had to now take an early retirement (ten years before he wanted to), thus taking us to numerous additional appointments to also apply for social security for disability. This was a year-and-a-half process. It's amazing, the documentation you must provide to prove you are disabled and cannot work in your field of work. Ultimately, it was finally approved after a year and a half's time, which was an absolute must for us. We had to have oxygen supplies delivered to the home: an oxygen maker and a portable tank that you can fill with oxygen from it. Robert ran a line from it so it could reach throughout the whole house. I found myself accidentally stepping on this routinely and pulling the hose off his face—not a fun process.

One day, I felt like I should see what this felt like for him, wearing a hose on your face. I wore it around the house while cooking, eating, showering, and dressing. Let me tell you this: it was not fun at all. And here is my husband, Robert, who never once complained about this or any other part of the process. The positive attitude and sense of humor that Robert carried with his illness was absolutely inspiring. When you watch someone struggle but not complain, it makes you see people and life differently. You come across people daily in your life who complain about trivial things; and honestly, you think you have no clue how good you have it every day—to which I say, "Take nothing for granted. You never know what life has in store for you or how well you will embrace and accept it."

I remember going to routine doctor appointments, telling my doctors the situation we were in, and being asked by one of my doctors if I was angry. Honestly, I never was. I found myself feeling compassionate about this situation and tried to put myself in Robert's shoes, thinking about how difficult it must be for a man with his pride to not be able to work or do the things he enjoys. I just kept telling myself, "We will survive," and I relied on my faith and constant prayer as well as the support of friends and family to make it through. I tried my hardest for him to not see my anxiety/acceptance of it all as well. I am sure there were days when my patience had run thin and when we grumbled at each other, especially in this first year. The first eight months of this journey I did not journal; however, I collected many quotes and, to this day, still read daily Bible verses and pray morning and night. I will center on all the quotes and music that helped me through later in the book.

I know Robert did not want to accept this whole ordeal. He failed to tell me he was smoking, and it delayed our process for an additional six months for transplant listing. He admitted it was the wrong thing to do, and when he finally accepted the severity of this condition, we were able to move forward with the whole process. Whether he realized it or not, he started taking better care of himself physically as far as eating, rest, exercise were concerned. The positive attitude was always there.

The new schedule took about a year for us to get used to, as now I was more "accepting" and "tolerated" our newly adjusted schedules. Now we are in the house together all hours, which—don't get me wrong—is not a really bad thing, just an adjustment. There was a delivery of an oxygen concentrator (loud). We first placed it in the bathroom, but it was too loud and hot. Then we placed it in the basement and fed the cord up through a vent, and this would be the permanent fixture (in the basement), with miles of cord to stretch throughout house. We had portable tanks for Robert to carry when he/we went anywhere and other large tanks for use, and again brought upstairs closer to his chair. In this whole process, there were many times I saw the frustration with Robert having a cannula in his nose and a tank on his shoulder, but he never voiced it. Even with his medical condition, Robert still did the dishes for me, ran errands, gassed up our vehicles, made the bed, cut the lawn, cleaned the gutters, and kept our vehicles maintained. Having a spouse with a medical condition is probably kind of like having a baby: it's new, it's scary, and you worry about injuring or making their condition worse in the romance department. Robert used to say, "If something happens, just dress me up nice in a suit and sit me up." And there is that sense of humor I love so much.

And here we were, eight months into the process, and there was a "family" meeting at the hospital. This was very informative and educational for all.

I believe it took family and friends a long time to accept and understand the process as well. People will be unsure about how to approach you or the loved one with the illness. They will ask questions, but it will take time and numerous interactions with them witnessing the person to realize how much of an impact it has on your lives. Even strangers will stare at you, which is so disrespectful. Someone with an illness that requires them to take in more oxygen experiences stress when preparing to go to a social event. You have to plan accordingly. Portable tanks will only last you so long. In the last eight years, we had to stay within four hours of the hospital because we were "on call," waiting for that lifesaving phone call. So there were no vacations outside that four-hour time frame. Forget about flying because that would be a hassle, and you need to keep the patient's medical history on you and know of a medical facility close by wherever you travel to.

Somehow, I never became angry about this. I just wanted to cherish each day with Robert no matter what we did. There were so many things that I know were hard for him to do, but he did them because he knew they made me happy—grilling on the BBQ, for instance; taking me for a drive in the muscle car with a stick shift; or fixing something in the house or outside of the house. He would pace himself because he knew that if he did, it would bring me joy. He has the heart of a lion, bigger than life—an inspiration.

One thing I learned is that social interaction was a huge part of this successful journey. As hard as it was for him at times with his breathing problem, he still agreed to go to parties or dinners we were invited to or I planned. This became a routine part of our lives monthly. I would make sure we had dinner with friends or family once or twice a month. The laughter and communication not only helped us as a couple still see that he could do normal things in the midst of chaos, but I also think it helped others really understand what he/we were going through. People began to ask questions and understand.

Let's make another thing clear also. Some never understand or try to understand and are just acquaintances in your journey. You really gain a lot of clarity in so many areas and truly realize who is genuine and who will be there for you. I am so grateful as we have had so many wonderful people in our lives. The support is unbelievable.

Another huge aspect Robert and I became involved in is the Henry Ford Hospital Lung Transplant Support Group. It meets once per month for two hours. We met people of all ages and nationalities with different health conditions that made them need more oxygen. Support meetings are crucial in any illness you are dealing with. These are people that are in the same boat as you who can relate and offer advice pre- and posttransplant. We learned something from every meeting we attended, and we continue to attend. I grabbed the bull by the horns and started to run the meetings early on by assisting the clinical psychologists and notifying people of the location, time, and speaker weeks before the meeting dates. I even had cards made to be placed on the transplant floor. I reached out to patients on the transplant lab floor and offered info even on appointment dates because they were scared to death in the process, just like us. We met people who were instrumental in Rob's growth and mine as well. There were things we learned from going year after year that helped us in the situations that arose at the time of surgery and afterward.

There are educated doctors, nurses, coordinators, Life Flight coordinators, dieticians, pharmacists, insurance specialists, and gift-of-life advocates who speak. As I write this, flooding through my mind are so many faces of people we have met over the years and memories of how much they enlightened our lives. Some are still with us, but many have passed, unfortunately. We will be forever grateful for the impact, knowledge, care, genuine kindness, and support they showed us. There were also a couple of gift-of-life symposiums at hospital honoring the donor families, which were very educational and emotional. From the first one we attended, I became a huge advocate, trying to educate people (even strangers) as much as I can on how important organ donation is.

As I continue through this chapter of acceptance, I will place some occasional happenings in here like this one that happened in January 3, 2009: Dad and Claudia phoned at 11:45 p.m. with a football question. This was one of the first times my heart dropped with a late phone call as of late, but lo and behold, it was not a call with donor notification. But hey, that's okay.

January 10, 2009

Dad and his friend Jack brought a treadmill over for Robert. What a great idea; we both used it!

January 23, 2009

Today Robert had an esophageal fundoplication. Five incisions to his stomach were made laparoscopically. This is a procedure he needed to have because of his stomach acid. They worried about the acid invading the lungs, so this procedure twisted the stomach to prevent the acid from coming up. Needless to say, at his first hospital stay, I was a wreck from seeing him in a bed, uncomfortable on a morphine drip… I left to go home and cried all the way home, just worried about the future, his health, and so much more to come. I came home, depressed, and bought an outfit for work online. Funny how shopping can make a girl feel a little bit better!

April 1, 2009

I was heavily into online schooling courses, appointments, and work; so I did not journal for four months—wow! However, on this day, Robert April-Fooled me and called the transplant pager. There's that sense of humor again!

June 15, 2009

This month's support meeting was very emotional. There was a pastor present; and so were both our nurse coordinators, the social worker, two gentleman who had transplants, one of the gentleman's wife/caretaker, and us. Today was the first time I shared and broke down how emotionally, mentally, and physically draining this whole process was. I told of how I admired Robert's strength, positive attitude, and sense of humor. I told them I had worked with patients for years and many different personalities and never met anyone quite like him. I also said he was an inspiration to all who knew him and that his courage through adversity was undeniable. I remember clearly one of our nurse coordinators, Patti, saying how humbling it was to listen to the patients and their spouses' stories. She was emotional, and I think I saw some emotions in Robert coming through that day when I shared. I am not sure at this point if he even realized the impact all of this had on our lives, but I have a feeling it was becoming more clear.

August 1, 2009

It was 9:00 a.m. on a Saturday, and the home phone rang… We were still in bed. Lauri, one of our nurse coordinators, left a message saying to call her. I got right up and called. She apologized profusely and said Robert's name was under the name of the woman they were trying to reach to transplant today! This was our first false alarm and my second! She felt pretty bad, and Robert said, "You are forgiven." Hahaha there is that sense of humor. She said, "I feel like such a schmuck!"

An Unknown Angel's Gift

Mid-August 2009

This was the day of our first meltdown… Quoting from my journal, "Robert seems like a lot weighing on his mind." I observed him frequently. I knew he worried about finances and the daily monotony of this disease, and not working and the changes weighed heavy on his mind. It was hard for me as a wife not to become worried or concerned. He was clearly upset. I can't imagine how hard it must've been for him. As a man, pride is a huge force. Sometimes we'd snap at each other over the stupidest stuff, and then it would all be good again. If you want to test a marriage, throw an illness of a spouse into it. You don't expect any of this in your young years of marriage; you might anticipate it happening after retirement or in your elder years. Being forced to address it while young and retire young must have been a huge burden on him, and yet he made no complaints. One day at work this month, someone asked me how he was, and I just broke down in tears. It's so hard to watch someone you love struggle with an illness. You feel helpless.

I don't think anyone can truly understand what it is like unless they experience it. It was a short, quick meltdown at work, but it happened. This was the beginning of many unexpected tearful times.

Whether you realize it or not, your emotions are running high. And having someone ask you about it early on when you are just so vulnerable and scared, when you don't know what to expect, and when you are on call… Every time the phone rang, especially if the number had a 313 area code, I'd wonder if that was "the call." You hear a song, and you become emotional.

Early in the process, every week, specifically the day after a support meeting, I would break down quietly at my desk at work while feeling scared to death, trying to process all the information we were learning, appear put together at work, and function like a normal human being. But inside, as I said, I was scared to death and trying to be the rock I needed to be for my spouse. Every day to this day, I pray for the strength to be a positive individual for my husband and for others around me. When going to numerous appointments and the hospital, you see things so differently, and you are so grateful. I just found myself becoming stronger and stronger and was always trying to reach out to make others feel better. You see so much sickness, negativity, and fear with people, and you just want to make it all right. Having a sense of humor as well as friends and family, again, will get you through all the emotions, as I frequently said at the meetings during this whole journey/adventure, which is like a roller-coaster ride.

That being said, let us not forget the first year Rob became listed. He had done what is called a fast-track testing. You name it, they tested it on him. Our lives were week after week of doctor appointments, tests, and my keeping close records of this. Robert never ceased to amaze me with his always great sense of humor and great attitude. He strengthened me as I watched him do what so many people do in an illness situation: they either become stronger and deal with it, or they become weaker and withdrawn. Robert became very involved in pulmonary and physical rehabilitation. The conditioning of muscles is very important to prepare your body for an intense operation. I cannot stress enough that this is one of the key factors we learned at the support meetings—to condition your body and exercise as much as possible to keep yourself healthy and prepared for when you get that call! This was a very trying month for us with many bumps in our attitude/outlook on things. Even with a positive attitude, you still will have bumps in the road, and you will argue over stupid, trivial things because you have that underlying stress. As I said, these types of medical situations will test your every resolve of your marriage; and you have to decide if you are strong enough to stay, fight it out, and make it worth it. Robert was worth it.

We were very impatient with each other at times, and really, it is all about accepting things and working through them. Everything isn't going to be in its place in your house. Remember, your schedules are different now, so you will have to adjust. That being said, the winter months are the most trying because there is not as much to do and you are under each other. You have to find a happy medium and have your own space even when in the house together. You must respect each other's space, treat each other with respect, and communicate. If you can do that, you will make it.

In a support meeting in August was our first Life Flight crew speaker (they pick up the organs for the recipient!). We were told Robert's name had come up but that he was not a good match. There was a low turnout today, but it was a very informative meeting.

We missed September's meeting—the first one we missed! Robert, Dad, and Jack were working on a new enclosure for the GTO, and things were going well. But I knew it was frustrating for Robert as he had to pace himself.

September 18, 2009

While I was still in the acceptance process, a coworker lent me a book on perseverance relating to cancer survivors. Her teenage daughter survived a rare bone cancer (there was a tumor in her leg), and I found her story to be very uplifting. Here is a quote from the book: "To fight passionately in the face of adversity is to achieve victory." Indeed.

October 1, 2009

Robert had some unidentified lung bacteria that they had been treating him aggressively for with thousands of milligrams of medication, which he finally was getting off, and then he had to deal with ear-ringing issues. These had been very stressful for him. He was still staying positive.

October 10 to November 1, 2009

They had the car port completed—great work by Robert, Dad, Jack, and Dad's friend Joe. It took a lot of hard work and patience, but they succeeded. He loved telling everyone about the building of the enclosure! He should feel proud. They all worked well together and succeeded!

Robert took me for a spin in the GTO. "Hopefully, someday," I quote from my journal, "he will have no breathlessness when shifts his car! The day I can look over and see him shifting, not getting winded, will be a true blessing!" I also wrote in my journal, "Hopefully, this will be next year," which would have been 2010.

The October meeting was the first meeting we had been to where Robert the only one waiting for a transplant. All attendees had their transplants already and were doing well. This was the point where I really took on helping with the groups and starting taking email addresses to notify people about the meetings and speakers. One of the attendees (Rob's brother's father-in-law) gave us some reading material and four tapes to watch regarding transplant.

The November support meeting was all about your diet and the fat content in foods. This was very informative. It may sound quite boring to you, the reader; however, it was an eye-opener to realize how many grams of fat are in the food we eat! Again, at this meeting, Robert was the only one still waiting for a transplant.

December 2009

We had now been listed for one year. Yes, we started the process in 2008. Robert was listed on December 2008, so it had now been a full year. And I felt we were at that acceptance point. I received a lovely bookmark from a coworker that said, "Dream. Believe. Succeed." Indeed.

To close this acceptance chapter, I would like to talk about the December meeting, our first Christmas dealing with the acceptance of Robert's illness together, and all we dealt with. The December meeting is the best one yet that we had been to. Everyone we have met since beginning the process was there. Everyone looked and felt great. I remember one spouse in particular (gearheads also) who talked about how wonderful it was to look over at her husband and picture him as a twenty-one-year-old again and healthy, and their daughter-in-law broke down in tears from being so happy also. There was another couple that was fourteen years out—inspiring! There was a pastor and his wife who were about to adopt a child. There was a thin, frail young lady who was wheelchair bound last year who was now doing great. There was an older gentleman who was so grateful for doing great, and his wife as joyful. There were two other women who were doing fabulously. Another gentleman we had come to know well was also doing well; he was very fit. Another couple who reached out to us waited three years and was doing well.

The whole pulmonary team of nurses and doctors was present, and everyone could not give them enough praise. And they were right. They were all gifted. Today, Robert shared about wanting to shift his muscle car without getting winded. I shared how proud I was of him. It was so hard to share at the meetings as I'd get so emotional from hearing all the stories and thinking of all we had been through. To see his struggles day to day was a hard process, and I just wanted him to have a new and better lease on life with no struggles!

Christmas Day, 2009—today the emotions of the last year caught up with Robert, and he broke down and cried. Granted, we had been short and quick to yell at each other over the stupidest things. Both of us were tired, stressed, and scared. But throughout this whole process—as I again stress—I was inspired by his strength in days of adversity. Deep down, it must've been a lot harder than anyone can imagine.

I know he probably didn't want to share his fear for fear of stressing me out more, but I am so glad he did. Him not being able to talk to his parents had to have been a huge issue as I know they were always there for him through everything in his life.

It's not easy for a man to open up about his feelings. I have only seen Robert cry a few times. I think this was a powerful cry he needed. I expressed how he could vent to me anytime, whether it be crying, screaming, venting, or just needing a good talk—whatever he needed to do to express his feelings. I know that the appointments, the thoughts and worries of the future, the blood draws, the breathing tests, the testing walks, the rehab, the monotony of the days, the not being able to work (which he loved), the listening to me talk every day, doing things for me, and just plain waiting for that call…

for a lifesaving surgery…must've played on his nerves every day. But he was never one to complain or talk much about it. I was not the patient, so how could I begin to even understand? I could just be there for support. The fact that he shared with me his thoughts and emotions meant the world to me, and it was a turning point. It was a sign of the acceptance of this disease.

This was a wonderful Christmas in spite of all we had been through. Robert bought so many nice gifts for me for Christmas, so many heartfelt gifts. He went all out. He loved the computer notebook I got him. I thought this would be a nice gift for him so that when he got hospitalized, he'd be able to go on the computer while he lay up in the hospital bed if he wanted to. We had family visitors that day and also talked with many on the phone.

To close my journal entry on this Christmas day, I wrote, "I truly hope 2010 brings better health for Robert because he deserves it. Mom B always said he was very special/unique, and she was right."

Chapter 2

Minute-by-Minute, Month-by-Month, and Year-by-Year Details

We must use time as a tool, not as a crutch.
—John F. Kennedy

THE SEASONS, HALLMARK HOLIDAYS, AND other holidays come and go so quickly. You feel as if you are in a cloud, going through the motions. The minutes, days, months, years…*tick tock*… Every time one would come, I would put up the decor, and I would think, *I wonder if we will get that call.* And the call never came… I thought, *I wonder when that call will come.* Then I put the decor away and wait for the next one. Some days, I thought it would never come. *Will Robert be one of those patients who is on death's door and in a hospital bed, waiting? God, I hope not.* You cherish every moment. You take pictures. You make memories. You pray for strength. The unexpected is so hard. You cannot explain the level of stress this situation puts on your life. It's not supposed to be this way. But you accept it; and you go through the motions minute by minute, month by month, and year by year.

Late 2008

This was a period of psychologist and social-work questioning extravaganza—background information, short- and long-term memory testing—and let's not forget we were reminded be sure to complete our directive paperwork! The years 2008 and 2009 are a blur of endless visits.

I remember vividly an early, cold day in January 2010. My boss was retiring at work, and we had an office retirement party for him. This was a particularly hard day for me because he gave a speech where he talked about his loss of family and how people "have" to retire. His speech made me think of my husband, Robert, and how he had to retire, and I became very emotional. It made for a very long day. All the thoughts and events from the last year or so came to an eruption. I did not speak personally to my boss that day. I took a later lunchtime. I came home as I did every day and vented about my day, and Robert listened as he always does and understood. He held me and gave me a massage. I am blessed. Those moments where you can just sit, talk, listen, and communicate are what marriage is all about. In spite of chaos, you find those moments to appreciate each other.

February 2010

On my birthday, Robert sent flowers to me at work, which he frequently has done since the beginning of our relationship. He made me dinner and dessert. Wow!

As the seasons continued to roll on. We did not have too bad of a winter this year. This month, there was hardly any snow—thank goodness. The winter months were so much more stressful on our relationship and went by so much slower. We were stuck inside. I know it was emotionally more draining for Robert, seeing me doing the things he wanted to do around the house.

The winter months will find you grumbling more at each other. You won't get out as much. As a woman, you'll learn to accept things around the house. Its more lived-in, and you just accept it because, really, it's all about the time you spend together. That means the most. I cannot stress again how important it is to make sure to schedule early dinners on weekends at least twice a month with family or friends. You need that sense of normalcy, acceptance, and laughter in your life in spite of what you are waiting for and going through.

On this month, we were told by Robert's pulmonary doctor, "You can wait two months for your next checkup! But as we rolled into March, we lost our beloved Gran. No words can describe this loss and how I felt. Yes, this book is about Robert, me, and the experience, but she played a huge part in our support system. We talked frequently, and she thought the world of Robert. She would come in, make us meals, and come with us to appointments for support. She knew how to listen and understand. She watched her daughter suffer with cancer and her husband suffer through an illness, and she was the strongest woman I knew. I went through anger, shock, dismay, and sadness with her loss. It was like someone ripped my heart out. Gran was my confidant. We talked, we laughed, we shopped, and we lunched. She understood me as no one could, and I her. It was as if someone pulled a rug out from under me. Yes, she lost her daughter at thirty-one years of age, and I was eight years of age. I had no memories of my mom, only what everyone told me. From what I understand, she was a truly amazing woman. I will cherish the memories I have of Gran forever. She touched everyone in a special way. While going through that loss, I would see birds and blue skies, hear a song, and think of her and the wonderful way she had with people. She was a truly genuine woman who brightened a room everywhere she appeared. I know she would not want me to continuously grieve but remember all the happy memories.

My brother Bill and I had a lot of heart-to-heart talks throughout the whole process and became closer, which I am grateful for. Robert became even closer to the family also. It was hard on him emotionally as well. We spent eight days in and out of the hospital. There was lots of driving, crying, and eating what we could. I ended up with a god-awful cold for two weeks.

You don't ever get over the loss of a loved one. Everyone grieves in different ways. Gran had a head injury. I pray she did not suffer. I know she would have wanted to have her organs donated; however, she never registered for it. The Lord welcomed her quickly and with no pain or suffering. My niece was with her in the hospital shortly before she passed. Her husband, mom, sisters, and brothers welcomed her, I am sure. During this whole process and in spite of Robert's health issues, Robert's support, love and guidance helped get me through. I hope I can always be as patient, kind, supportive, and loving to him.

One day at work a few months after Gran's passing (on Mom's birthday), I was having a really hard time that day and looked out the window. I saw three geese under a pine tree. The sun, grass, and lighting were nice, so I decided to take a picture. The picture showed three white figures and no geese. Before I took the picture, I thought, *That is Gran, Grandad, and my mom.* It was a beautiful, heartfelt moment. I truly believe our loved ones are around us frequently. I like when my brother and I have heart-to-heart talks. It means a lot, and siblings should always know they can confide in one another even though it can be a painful process.

April 2010

Dad and I painted the interior of the house, every room. It was an enjoyable, well-needed, exhausting process! It was a "working" vacation! This is the only April entry because, as I put it in my journal, "I am scattered!"

You go into an entirely different mindset. I created large binders with all the doctors' names, numbers, and locations. And let's not forget insurance issues, which we will discuss later as we talk about the experience day by day, month by month, and year by year.

An Unknown Angel's Gift

In the eight years we waited, Robert had many illnesses that sometimes spanned a whole weekend or a whole week. They involved fever, chills, body aches, cough, congestion, and water retention, thus involving more doctor appointments, which resulted in added stresses and questions. They told us there were colonies of bacteria in Robert's lungs that were not active but that nodules could form, and they said heavy doses of antibiotics would be needed and instructed us to watch for symptoms that sounded horrifying. Seven illnesses of this sort happened in 2008, a wonderful colonoscopy and a couple of illnesses happened in 2009, and three illnesses happened in 2010—one of which lasted four weeks. There were a couple of illnesses in 2011 and 2012. In 2013–2015, ironically, there were not as many bugs, but his breathing got worse. Let us not forget that throughout this whole process, they tested every part of his body for everything, from head to toe.

There are seventeen floors at the hospital we go to, and we have seen every one of them but one. Throughout this whole process, we were constantly going in with samples from Robert's cough and lab blood draws and to do walking and breathing tests every month as well as attend the support groups monthly.

I remember distinctly a call we received one day in 2010 from one of the nurse coordinators. The nurse said that one of his scans showed a nodule. Ironically, it was something that was mentioned to us in an earlier appointment. And then came a new test with radioactive dye to thoroughly look at this. Most likely, this was another bacterial colonization infecting his lung again; there was always a positive fungus—an unidentified mold or growth—growing in his contaminated, diseased lungs. When we would get these calls, we would have to compile all our questions and wait and worry until the next appointment where they could show us the x-rays and scans and tell us the reasoning behind what kind of medication or treatment they recommend. Robert was always compliant and did whatever they suggested.

Within two months' time, in the dead of summer, the doctors now said there were *two* nodules on the left and *one* on the right.

They were less than half a centimeter big, and there was no cancer, just a bacterial infection again. Robert had to start yet another course of medications. All I could think was *My poor husband,* but he had always been a good sport through it all. And as for me, my anxiety attacked in private. But I never read too much into my anxiety. He was my main concern, and by power of prayer and support, it was all doable.

Within one week of taking the medications, Robert felt like crap, but he never complained. He just continued to be a great husband, being helpful to me around the house and making me laugh, all the while pushing my buttons—but not intentionally! As we approached our wedding anniversary date, we got a call from the doctor to stop the medication as the infection was not what they had expected. There are many times throughout these circumstances when you question, "Is my loved one a test sample…a lab rat…for unanswered medical questions out there?" Obviously, it all is a learning experience in medicine, but it is just so scary when you experience it all. There are so many unanswered questions along the way. It is all so terrifying.

While we were going through this process, I came across a writing in one of my grandmother's Scripture books that read as follows: "We often think of hope as something hazy and intangible, a vague optimistic feeling that has little real use in this world, but in reality, hope is a practical thing. It is the light that leads us forward, the inspiration that encourages us to act, to create, to move ahead. Not only does Christ guide us through the darkness of this world; he is also the beacon of hope that points the way toward eternity. If we have no eternal hope, then we will live our lives in darkness, afraid to step out and love." And every day, I kept telling myself, "Robert will get his lungs soon." Keep the faith. Keep pushing forward. Keep your social calendar active to keep the sanity in both of you.

Two years into this process, I started reading a book about caregiving and decided at that time that I was going to write a book one day based on our encounters. Throughout this process with his being in and out of infections, it was increasingly frustrating for us. The monotony of it all would wear heavy on both of us. I would always describe it as a roller-coaster ride of emotions. I prayed constantly for his new lungs, better health for him, and a better life for us. I believe 2010 was one of the hardest years as they were constantly testing my husband with x-rays, labs, and CT scans to follow these so-called nodules and infections. They were treating him with aggressive antibiotics that made him experience nausea, dizziness, and body aches. After two months of this, the infectious disease specialist phoned to say, "Good news, the bacteria is nonspecific and one that rarely causes infection. Stop all medications!" This was the best news ever. At the next visit, the transplant doctor said that the other injectable medications the infectious doctor recommended were not necessary. After more tests and CTs, we were told that the nodules were much better, and the question was "Is it from the medication regimen, or was there another reason?" The physician said, "Let's get another CT and see the doctor in a month or two."

Two months later, Robert was sick again (these details to you as the reader may seem unnecessary, but not to someone going through it). Think of all the day-to-day stress involved (e.g., "Let's start the meds," "Let's stop the meds," "Let's run the test," "Let's not run the test," "Call us back in a day if things worsen," etc.). There were some questions at this point after I had a phone conversation with the nurse. She said, "Start the meds again and cancel the scans."

I said, "We just went through six weeks, and a CT is already scheduled."

She proceeded to tell me that the nodules were back.

I asked if the whole team was present at the meeting recently, and she said yes and that they made a collective decision as well as the surgeon. She was going to let them know we opted not to start the meds, do the CT next week, and still see the doctor (mind you, we have been waiting for weeks to see the doctor and discuss all the recent issues).

Throughout reading about this whole process, you must also take into account that I, as the spouse, am the one talking to all the nurses and doctors, relaying Robert's feelings, and discussing the plans of treatment. And in light of this episode with the nodules on his lungs, the aggressive medications and how crappy he felt during the whole process just made my blood boil because one process led to more and more questions. So I distinctly remember this visit. The lung specialist and infectious bacteria specialist were present. We were two years into this wait, mind you. There were many questions asked including how common it was for lung transplant patients to have the infections he had, and they said they were extremely common. They showed us the scan and stated that they would not biopsy them unless they became larger or presented an issue. They still had not identified the bacteria; the results always came back negative or unknown. After this visit, we did feel better about the situation.

After another month down road, the infectious disease specialist called and said the results came back positive but that it was an unidentified bacteria, so he said they would not treat it. Another month passed, and lo and behold, they informed us they would give Robert Prednisone. And also, their consensus was to restart the three awful medications that made Robert feel like crap, and more CTs and blood work followed in the future. One week later, they identified the bacteria, and now they said, "Do not take the three medications." And we waited for the next call.

How about all these details? At this point, I would hope you, my reader, are not bored by detail after detail, to express the enormity of the stress that one goes through week by week and month by month. You never know what to expect, all the while still knowing that one of those calls could be the call you're waiting for—to get a transplant!

The following week, they said, "We will treat." The next week, they said, "We will not treat." They then said that because Robert was a transplant patient, the infection can be severe after surgery if it was still present. This was a very rare bacterial organism, and wanted it treated correctly. So coming up on holidays and the word was "We will treat this aggressively, and there are possible GI side effects, tendon issues, and eye issues. We will treat it, and hopefully, we'll need six to eight weeks of negative cough sputum with no bacterial growth." They were doing extensive research on lung transplant infection cases and medication regimens in this regards, which is what they told us. After three weeks on the medication, this time, Robert had a bad taste in his mouth and heartburn. We followed up, and lo and behold, all samples came back negative!

The next year, Robert got bad colds, cough, and chest congestion. Antibiotics and Prednisone were given to him yet again. Also, at this time, Robert had allergies that erupted. We saw an ear, nose, and throat specialist. A vocal cord dysfunction was seen. We were educated on this as well as the ringing in his ears; and yet again, there came more tests, more doctors, and more medications. It was a never-ending battle and a learning process. After a year of all of this, the medications were stopped.

The next six months of this and the second year of being listed were a blur. As each day passed, I became more and more concerned about Robert's chest congestion. We continued the doctor appointments and kept attending the support meetings. Each season would come and go so quickly. I would get out our home decorations and stay in the spirit of things. I'd keep a positive outlook and be the rock that my husband needed to get through this roller-coaster ride of emotions and appointments while always expecting the unexpected, not ever sure of what each day might bring. We got a phone call from a number with the 313 area code and realized it was just to confirm an appointment, ask us a question, or an insurance case management worker. Let's not forget Robert wore the "pager" the hospital supplied for two years, replacing the batteries, only to not get that call. Oh, and he April-Fooled me twice with it! After this year, Robert quit wearing the pager and told them to call either of our cell numbers.

As I said early on in this chapter, the winters were the hardest. The days were full of monotony. It was cold out. The days were dark and dreary. Those were the worst. I'd worry, and my thoughts would be relentless. The worries were endless. We'd snap at each other over stupid, silly things because boredom was setting in. He hated seeing me shovel, snow-blow, and take out the trash. The neighbors stepped up and took care of the snow for us 90 percent of the time. It did bother me that Robert got too winded from doing these things, and I knew it bothered him. I tried not to pry too much into his feelings about all of this. Some days, I could really see the disgust and the many other emotions he, as the person going through it, must have felt. This is why I stress how important it is to keep your social calendar as busy as possible. Spend time with friends and family. Talk, laugh, and share. They will ask questions and become educated on a serious situation. The more time that passes, the more they'll also understand how hard it appears to be.

Our family and friends saw Robert stopping to catch his breath after enjoying a nice meal, walking, talking, and walking to his truck. They saw him or me running out to switch oxygen tanks. They became more and more interested and learned of the things we were going through. I can say that having the support of your friends and family is a huge part of a successful journey in waiting for a transplant. They love and support you, see your struggle, and know it is real. You will learn quickly which friends are fearful of it, cannot make the time for it, and just plain don't get it. You will learn quickly which friends really are your friends and not just acquaintances. They will call and ask how you and he/she are. They are genuine. This is an important part of growing in this process as you learn who you can depend on. Here is a quote for this portion of the process: If you want to learn, you will learn, accept, let go of fear, and just keep living.

2011

As we began the third year of this process, I did not journal the winter months. Go figure. It is shocking, but I am sure I just kept myself extremely occupied and busy. At this point, we were told that Robert had a sinus tach and would need to see a cardiologist yet again and have more echo/EKG testing. In April 2011, there was a colonization of infectious bacteria present. We got through it yet again, and Robert had a nasty head/chest cold for ten days in May of this year (2011). And then in August/September, things were "perfect"—no problem visit. In October, they told us he had no antibodies. In November, his blood pressure skyrocketed after his walking test, and his oxygen dropped to 71—very scary. They wanted more cough sputum. It was mesmerizing how, at the end of nearly all my journaling day by day, I wrote, "Come on, new lungs, new lease on life, for him/for us!" I was happy it was starting to feel like summer. It skipped spring, but we did not mind.

As we came into June 2011, however, Robert caught another bug that gave him a nasty cough/congestion/throat issue for three weeks. He was put on antibiotics and would undergo yet more labs again and another round of Prednisone! We missed a few events, and I knew this bummed Robert out. But he was quite ill. In these summerlike months, Robert did strive to make sure our gutters were cleaned and the yard beautifully cut. These were two home things he enjoyed, and I knew it was not easy on him with the awkwardness of the portable oxygen tank, which needed to be lugged along as he worked. But he made the best of it, and I assisted as best as I could, working well together. Everyone knows that there are some things around a house a man just knows and does better. Again, as I look at the end of a journal page, I see that I wrote, "I pray for Robert's good health and well-being."

As we continued in the month of June, I was letting work stress get to me, according to my journaling. I mention work because, as you know, it is a major part of everyone's everyday life and well-being. It is something you have to do. The day-to-day drama, blah-blah-blah, was getting to me. Someone ranted about their recent wonderful vacation on a cruise and how excellent it was, which just kinda felt "in your face." We hadn't gone on a vacation in years and could not take a long vacation outside of a four-hour mark. And again, as I wrote in my journal, it was time for Robert's surgery. He deserved it. I deserved it. We deserved it. At this point, it was the end of June, and we still did not have the muscle car out yet. And now, even the summer days were monotonous. I knew Robert was aggravated with the oxygen and chose not to get the muscle car out as it was a big job to do a step-by-step process. And again, I wrote in the journal on every page at the end of every entry, day by day, month by month, "I want Robert to feel better, to have new lungs." Interestingly, I wrote that being home, taking care of Robert, would be a much-needed, much-improved attitude adjustment for me!

As I look at the beginning of my July entries, my first sentence in the journal is "I am hanging on by a thread!" Everything was getting to me. I must not have been exercising or doing enough yoga. I was venting about doing all the calling to people and wanting to see them more often. I tend to worry too much about things…and I missed my gran. We could talk about anything. Well, I made it. We made it.

Here we were, going into August, and Robert gained seven pounds. His follow-up appointment this month went very well. And again, I wrote, "We just wait and wait and wait." We did get car out and went on a cruise. I so wanted him to just feel better. And here is a fortune from a fortune cookie for us: "The best times of your life have not yet been lived!"

August 2011 was the month of retaining water! And now we came upon another really emotional and educational support meeting with the Life Flight crew in September of this year, 2011. Many questions arose about hospitals and how they are affiliated with transplant programs. The fact came up that it was mandatory that all hospital contact the United Network for Organ Sharing when there was a brain-dead patient. The Life Flight gentleman mentioned how they might get ten to twenty offers a day with organs. We were told today that our organ offer would probably be an out-of-state offer since there were not enough registered donors in Michigan for Robert's criteria. The offers that arose had been for all petite people apparently! And the next season was fast approaching… Fall—that meant leaves, hot cocoa, boots, blankets, and naps! I routinely journaled how anxious I was for Robert to feel better, to breathe better. This month, they wanted him to have labs to check his antibodies to clarify if they were present. I was praying not another headache for us to endure as far as more lengthy tests or procedures for Robert.

I did not journal anything the month of October, which brings us to November 2011. Robert saw his initial primary pulmonologist this month as well as the infectious disease doctor who specialized in lung infections. Robert has raspiness in his chest, so a course of Prednisone was prescribed. Robert was feeling more and more winded, and the specialists told us, "This is not uncommon." That day, during Robert's required six-minute walk, his stats dropped quite low, and it was very scary. During these quick falls in stats with exertion, his neck would feel tingly, his fingers would look purple, and he'd feel lightheaded. You could see his body trying so hard to get oxygen to his brain all his other organs. How scary that was not only for him (but mind you, he will never show this; he is one tough cookie); imagine the fear in me as I watched him struggle at each and every one of these appointments but show strength as a man and do what the doctors wanted him to do. Talk about admiration. Seeing a man try so hard to fight this horrible monster of a disease trying to take hold of him. We did see a couple of people that day in the transplant program who were doing well, which was very inspiring to us. To see others working hard and doing what they were supposed to, to get to where they hope to be someday brought me to a quote one of our favorite people we met through the transplant program told us one day: "Hope and confidence do more good than medicine." A couple of years into this, the insurance issues began to be quite interesting, to say the least. That, my friends, will be discussed in another chapter in detail.

And we come to December 2011. We did not attend the hospital luncheon this year. We had a very, very busy month, but it was also very enjoyable with our families, who made sure we had very nice and enjoyable holidays together. Family makes every day worthwhile with their support, love, and joy. Seeing the little ones' excitement and faces brings so much happiness.

And as we come into December 30 of the new year, Robert became quite sick. We hoped 2012 would bring more good health for him, more happiness, and more *hope*.

2012

The year 2012… Wow, as I look back, I did not journal or share my thoughts on paper, which is shocking. But like a suspenseful novel or dramatic movie, I can picture the many appointments and fears we faced. I remember this year having many scares at Robert's appointments. His required six-minute walks were quite bad with his O_2 dropping to the sixties. Picture this once again: purple fingers on your spouse and them telling you they are lightheaded but want to keep pushing forward. This is the kind of person Robert is—so motivated, positive, and strong—and yet again, I was scared to death but was putting up a strong front for his sake because you cannot look weak or show your anxiety. You do not want it to add to the already hard journey they are trying to tackle. Again, as we approached a new year, Robert's blood pressure skyrocketed at a doctor visit, and his heartrate increased dramatically with activity/a walk at a visit to the doctor's office.

The year 2012 was a major year of research on the bacteria growing in Robert's lungs and recent studies pertaining to the types of bacteria and types of medicines. The head doctor talked about the different drugs used posttransplant at the doctor visits and always reviewed all test results and went over how Robert currently was feeling.

In the midst of dealing with all the stress of his health and day-to-day grind, we did take the muscle car out a lot (what a great stress reliever, taking a drive through the park). I also continued to make sure that we spent a lot of time with family and friends, just laughing, living, and having many heart-to-heart talks.

I remember thinking this was a relatively good year with not much to complain about. Why complain? When you watch someone struggle, it does no good to complain or be negative. You have to see the positive in every situation. This is something I really learned throughout this whole journey. No one can really understand what an ill person or their loved ones are going through if they do not live it. You have to look for the positive, look to faith to guide you through, and just be thankful. We met many who had failed marriages, but not us. We made the best of this situation that had turned our lives upside down. Sometimes you can look at a person with an illness and think, *Oh, they are not that bad.* But deep down, emotionally, you do not know their pain or thoughts every day. You don't know how scared they must be.

I write these thoughts to try and hopefully make people realize the sincerity and genuine care loved ones need when they are going through an illness. Reach out and ask them how they are because they need you to. Take them to lunch. Compliment them. Enrich their lives with laughter. Show how much you truly care.

As we continued this journey, we met more and more people needing support going through the same thing as us. It is so helpful to share with others and know you are not alone. Do not be afraid to not only share with your close family and friends but also go to support groups. We went to groups outside of our regular hospital group, and we learned at each and every one of them. At the end of 2012, Robert's oxygen dropped to 61 after his walk—very dangerous.

Early 2013

As we approached 2013, I did not, again, journal the winter months. Shocking. I am sure I was trying to keep as busy as I possibly could, and as I have said time and time again, the days just flew by even in the midst of watching Robert's health deteriorate. In January, we are already faced with the following after the doctor visit: Robert's heart was not enlarged, but they said there were calcifications of the thoracic aorta and coronary arteries, which they would watch. Again, the upper-right lobe nodule was mentioned, and so were the severe bilateral bullous:

> There is a new noncalcified nodular density superior segment of right lower lobe adjacent to 8 mm × 9 mm × 14 mm, as well as emphysema and left basilar bullae and the small area in the

upper lobe noticed. New nodule 13 mm which is suspicious for neoplastic process. CT may be helpful for further evaluation, more appointments to schedule for them to watch these nodules that are apparently stable, but yet we have to worry about them.

As we look at March 2013, my first words in my journal are "This is very stressful for us!" And then I say we were just "*fine*." And then I proceed to say, "I can tell the stress is getting to Robert." I said this every time after the winter months have passed.

Please hear me when I say you must keep busy with friends and family because I know the monotony of the days drove him nearly mad with the cold, quiet, dark winter days of being bound inside on oxygen. Can you imagine how frustrating it must have been for him? I am sure he could say many choice words in this book. In the winter months, he contradicted things I said, and I snapped back. Illnesses test your marriage. I'd try to stay so patient, calm, happy, and positive. He'd go off on me. I'd think it was something stupid, and then I'd react. We were both guilty of it. All couples are, but when you throw an illness into the mix, it is tenfold. When it happens, naturally, it sucks! Again, you must stay busy; too much quiet time is not good. It will drive you both mad. You must have trusted friends (true friends, not just acquaintances) you can spend time with together and apart. It's the best for your own health and well-being. And I came across a journaling item that says, "I just pray for strength for him and for me, for us. I want the best for him." And then I journaled that I wanted surgery for him, a good recovery, more activity, and more life because we had a lot more living to do! We saw a news story that day about the Renaissance walk in Downtown Detroit, and we said to each other, "We will do that someday!"

In March of this particular year, Robert was very crabby, which was highly unusual for him! His cough sputum grew three different bacteria! Argh! The doctors were saying that the vessels to his lung and heart were working harder. His score increased, which moved him up on the waiting list. The recent CAT scan showed a spot on the top right part of his lung, which they wanted to watch closely and discuss with all of their pulmonary team. Robert saw his regular pulmonologist in April 2013 (the same one who referred him to a transplant team in Downtown Detroit). He did indeed mention the nodule at top of Robert's right lung also and stated, "You would not want a biopsy right now." He dropped one of his medications to a very low dose, which, in turn, was returned to a higher dose by the team relatively quickly as he was not doing well at all with breathing and day-to-day activities on a low dose. Continuous CAT scans were done this year to watch the nodules on his right lung, which remained stable. There was an incident where Robert had to see a cardiologist again as there was a sharp pain in his shoulder that traveled down his arm and switched sides. Numerous tests were done yet again, although Robert was quite used to what seemed to be continuous tests on a frequent basis. Muscle relaxers and pain medicine were given, nothing was shown on the x-ray, and there were no clots on ultrasound. Robert's hands felt tingly from lack of oxygen; they felt Robert might have been arthritic! Numerous follow-ups after with the team revealed things to be stabilizing again as well as good blood pressure, echoes, walks, and labs.

A six-millimeter superior-segment lower-right lobe nodule remained unchanged from January 2013, but new from June 2011. We continued to follow up. There were no other significant nodules. Robert's extensive bullous emphysema remained unchanged. And you were yet again told when to follow up next time.

Oh, and let's not forget the blood gas analyses done twice yearly for Robert for eight years. And regarding the heart caths, echoes, x-rays, bone density tests, CAT scans, six-minute walks, pulmonary function testing, and numerous labs, UNOS must be kept up to date every six months with them. That computer must show current readings for listings all over the states so when that offer comes, the information is current. Regarding keeping up with all the medications and insurance billings/payments, the insurance and billing issues are enough to drive you out of your mind. I swear I spent every lunch hour on the phone, scheduling appointments or questioning billing matters. That is a full-time job. I was not about to expect my husband to call on insurance issues when he needed to concentrate on staying sane, trying to catch his breath with daily activities.

April 2013

Oh, how I hated dark, rainy, drab days; no sunshine made everything that much harder to deal with. Robert was continuing to do his pulmonary and physical rehabilitation to help keep things as healthy as possible for when we get that call. We continued attending the support meetings; they always went well but made me more emotional, especially the next day. A gentleman that we knew well had some heart issues, and we went to visit him in the ICU. What an eye-opener, walking around the ICU and then seeing this kind-hearted, wonderful person in bed with tubes. It made me think of how someday, I would see my husband in bed with tubes and fighting hard in recovery.

May to June 2013

May and June were busy with CT scans, heart caths, walks, and blood gas analyses at the hospital. The sixth-month marks were always very busy with appointments/tests for Robert and more worrisome as we awaited the results. Luckily, all results came out normal.

On another note, this summer, Robert and I had many heart-to-hearts, and he was getting a clearer understanding of my thoughts and sensitivity based on my childhood and why I react to things the way I do—with such compassion and understanding. We saw a comedy movie, and it was so good to just stop and laugh together. Whenever you go through any kind of added stress, laughter is such good medicine! It's so easy to become aggravated with the everyday stressors, but Robert has a way of making me laugh and easing my stress in any situation, which is a true gift if you stop and think about this situation: waiting…and waiting…and waiting…for that phone call that did not come. You have short fuses and snap at each other over stupid things on some days, and any fun activities can break the monotony of that waiting day in and day out. Laughter is the best medicine.

May to November 2013

There were multiple doctor visits in May, June, September, October, and November. One in particular in June was very scary. Robert's blood pressure was 136/66 before his required six-minute walk at his pulmonary visits. After his walk, his blood pressure shot up to 149/104. He rested, and then upon arriving to see the doctor, his blood pressure was then 132/66. There were more issues with his required sputum specimens, and he got sent home again with yet more cups for testing, more labs, another echo, and another CT order. And yet in another visit in particular in September of this year, his oxygen dropped to 84 before the doctor visit and after testing and all other changes. Fortunately, there were no changes on his CT, his "spiro blows" were stable, and his labs and cultures were all good. But they were sending more cups home with us to bring in December when we would do the dreaded blood gas analysis at that time of the follow-up.

Let me not forget a very frightening evening—the evening of October 10—when Robert had a sharp pain that traveled down his shoulder to his arm and into leg, switching sides from left to right. He had no chest pain or increase in breathing difficulty, and he took a Vicodin to rest. He felt tingly on October 11, so we went to a facility in Dearborn and also Henry Ford, which had good cardiology and emergency departments. And they did an ultrasound and x-ray. Robert stated that the pain felt like it was in his bones, not muscles. His blood pressure was 151/77. They found no clots. They stated that it was an arthritic issue and dispensed muscle relaxer and Vicodin. It was so hard to watch Robert in pain in addition to his breathing problem. We were told to follow up with his primary care doctor and then discharged. We left, and I worried. Nothing showed up on the x-rays or ultrasound. The pain subsided over time, but this was just another one of the many additional doctor visits we did not need! Thank goodness they found nothing, however.

December 2013

Here we were in December 2013 and going to our routine Henry Ford doctor visit. Robert's blood pressure was 134/90, and when he did their six-minute walk, it jumped to 176/95. He used 3 liters of oxygen today; he was having a hard day. His blood pressure was all over today too, and they kept checking. It was 165/95 after a walk then 179/84 before the doctor visit. These numbers may seem irrelevant to you as you read them, but I sat in the hallway as I did at every visit with Robert and watched him walk with the nurses, struggle, and push himself. Inside I was scared for him and for us, but I knew he would push himself and do everything he needed to do, always compliant and doing all the tests they required of him for them to have all their required numbers for their records and to update the UNOS (United Network for Organ Sharing) file on the computer. As I mentioned before, this gets updated methodically every six months as they must have these numbers on file so when or if they look and send out offers to potential patient recipients, facilities can see the scores of each patient. Robert always stayed between 30–40 percent, which kept him lower on the waiting list; but we knew that the longer the wait, the better medicine got, and the more they learned from each patient getting a transplant.

As I sat there while writing this, I remember how the days and months passed by so quickly; and I wondered how we ever got through all the agonizing appointments, insurance issues, and numerous additional "scares" throughout the whole process. I will remind you that the key factors are the following: support from family and friends; times of laughter that give us strength; my journaling throughout this whole process helped me; and my watching Robert getting up every day and attacking the day with enthusiasm, sarcasm, and strength. His strength gave me strength and still does. I can see what people mean when they say that when see a loved one going through a difficult process, it makes them stronger. I think this process can make or break a person. In our case, it made us stronger as human beings and as a couple. I have never had more respect for a human being as I did or do for my husband. As a caregiver, you watch them struggle day after day, month after month; wonder how they are coping; and hope that you can stay, look, or act strong for them, going about your day with strength even though you feel scared and unsure. I would think of how he must feel about wearing oxygen every day and being forced to slow down because of an illness that has taken hold of him. You never forget watching someone go through this. It's very difficult. I would still try to muster all my strength myself to still make each and every day and activity count, even a simple one, because I was more in love with this man than ever. And I was grateful he was in my life and able to do the things he still could in spite of this debilitating disease trying to bring him down.

We had been waiting for five years now for that call…that still had not come. We brought out the holiday decor again and then put it away. We celebrated and grasped for another year of watching, waiting, and hoping. Robert had more better days than down days. We had a new great-grandniece and great-grandnephew.

2014

Here were are in 2014. Wow. I note that I made very few journal entries for three months. Here is an inspiring journal entry for January 1, 2014: "Upon my awakening in Robert's arms, he says, 'Happy New Year,' and plants a kiss on my face!" These are the moments I treasure even though the cabin fever was unbelievable. And on March 1, 2014, my first three words in the journal entry are "Stress, stress, stress." I was driving the truck every day (except on those days I say, "What a blessing it is to have a husband who will drive me to work on an eight-inch snow day") as I did when weather was treacherous in Michigan during winter at times, and I knew Robert had a worse case of cabin fever than I did.

It was mid-January, and we had twelve inches of snow already in Michigan. Each week was nonstop, relentless cold wind; it was exhausting weather. I journaled when I could, and I knew my non-complaining husband was getting worse. The weather outside blew and was so cold. There was so much snow; it fell nonstop. I journaled, "Cannot wait for spring to break so we get a break, and we can get out more together." I had an adult beverage every night!

And then we got a horrible blow: a gentleman very close to us who was a huge mentor had died. He gave us so much support and knowledge and had a wonderful spirit. He would be greatly missed. It was a very sad time. And I see two blank pages in my journal. I guess I was speechless and just plain sad, mourning with Robert over this great loss but also reflecting on what a wonderful soul this man was. He was so giving and so loved by so many. We are grateful we had him in our lives.

March 2014

Doctor visit was a good visit. Robert's blood pressure was 141/78, his oxygen saturation was good today, and he had good labs and weight. We were instructed to get another echo (which didn't seem to be consistent any more) and were told that we would do another walk on the next visit. We were also told to see regularly a pulmonologist to get more pulmonary rehabilitation orders and Xanax refills (which Robert takes at bedtime due to his tinnitus [ringing in the ears]). We saw a regular lung doctor also, as instructed, which we do once a year to keep that relationship going other than the pulmonologist team we see for his listing and follow-up.

April to June 2014

April, May, and June had their ups and downs. Spring had sprung; however, Robert and I were still testy with each other, flying off the handle easily. Think about it: five years of monthly doctor visits, insurance calls, and pulmonary rehabilitation; his watching me try to do so much; and his health decline causing him to do less than he wanted to. These would wear on anyone's nerves, but we both kept pushing on because we have to. I journaled how much we enjoy time with the family or friend gatherings.

Oh, how much we needed the summertime. Gardening, driving in my convertible, reading, and yoga are therapeutic releases for me. I love the mornings when we awaken, hug, kiss, talk, and really listen to each other and just enjoy each other's company. I note a nice summer day in May when Robert, in spite of feeling crappy, fixed a broken part on my Mustang and had it washed and detailed. We cooked out; did yard work; and cruised around together, just talking and running errands together. It was another day of me being thankful.

Another meaningful event this month was when we attended a beautiful outdoor wedding together. When you see the magic of true love, it makes you appreciate yours even more. As we approached Robert's birthday, I was able to get Grand Prix tickets "Happy Birthday" and "Start Your Engines." It is so refreshing to go to an event and have the staff treat you with courtesy and extra care. We had close seating and great transport throughout the whole day, which made it less stressful on Robert to enjoy an event. We also took a few days to go up north and relax. The weather was fantastic, and the company even better. The food, cocktails, beach, and scenery were all great; it was a much-needed getaway.

Journaling inspirational quotes helps me as well. I will mention those in a later chapter. Positive energy or quotes can make a difference in how you approach your day. It is inspiration. It gets you through a difficult process at that moment. Don't take life for granted. I note that I journaled how much I love the quiet, tender, gentle moments we can share. I cannot stress enough that when going through a difficult time, take time to enjoy the gentle, soft quietness of the early morning when you awake. Say a prayer. Be thankful.

July to August 2014

With summer, there was not as much journaling, but we had a wonderful anniversary in July. We went to many car shows in the months of July and August. It's always a great outing for us with all the cars and smiling faces. "I cannot wait to walk the car shows and see Robert shift the GTO for the first time without oxygen," I wrote in my journal. That would be the best mood lifter ever. We also had many dinner date nights with friends and family. We had some boating time with friends also. As we approached September, we just might be home, relaxing more, with less car shows and fall approaching. I noted this had been a very stressful work year for me (but I was promoted to administration) in addition to Robert's health issues, but I continued to pray for strength in the mist of the rain. In the clouds, I knew there was a rainbow. We would see that rainbow, sunshine, and light at the end of this long hard tunnel of life. I told myself this often.

September 2014

We had a routine doctor visit with the transplant team at the main hospital in Downtown Detroit. Things were stable and progressing (this we knew), but we stayed faithful and positive on this journey!

October to December 2014

Fall had come and gone, and it was now a crisp winter day—dry but no snow. There hardly was snow at all. We had been able to still get out more due to this, which, of course, helped our mood and our attitudes toward each other.

October and November came and went. The days just flew so fast like a jet airplane flying overhead, a passing storm, a quick kiss, or a child's personality changing ever so fast—not sure where that just came from.

December had arrived, and the holidays with family were simply wonderful.

January 2015

And the year was 2015. On January 1, 2015, Robert asked me to comb out his long hair after showering today. He never did this, but I knew how much of a struggle a shower (which all of us who can breathe take for granted) was. We went out for many dinners this month. I noted the way people stared at Robert's oxygen at times, and it infuriated me. I wanted to say, "Take a picture" or maybe "You could not judge" and ask kindly, "Why?" No one knows why people may have or are a certain way due to a medical condition, but when you think about the person that has the condition and how long it must take them to accept it and be able to go out and feel comfortable, it's a difficult process. I rarely noticed over the years people staring, but sometimes I did. And that's when I grabbed him close (as I didn't know if he noticed), and I hoped they'd see the love that two people could share even with a health condition. I also remember this one time dancing on the dance floor with Robert and thinking of how much of a nuisance it must have been for him to carry that oxygen tank, but he did it. He did it for me because that is the kind of person he is.

Due season was coming. It was when he would no longer have to carry that tank on his shoulder, have that cannula in his nose with a cord, and worry about if he had enough oxygen to pack when we went somewhere. Due season—when Robert would be able to do things that made him happy and not rely on a tank to get enough oxygen to his lungs to function.

February 2015

We had a cold (yuck), but we still went to a movie and lunch! Again, he made sure to make me happy.

March to August 2015

Amazingly enough, I did not have many journal entries, and what journaling I did write reiterated how frustrated, irritated, and aggravated I knew Robert was getting with each day that passed… I could tell his nerves were wearing thin. I did my best to stay positive and keep it real. How many times have I said, "I just want him to feel better"? We just continued on with the doctor appointments, the medical bills, the frustration, and the positive attitude. We had to.

Here is an exciting piece of news. Robert bought us a new muscle car (an automatic): a 1972 Camaro. It was beautiful. It was fun. It was necessary. It exemplified our love for cars, and to see him smile even more makes my days better. We took it to a few shows with it being easier for him to drive, not having to use a stick. He says this car is for me. Wow, what a guy! Yes, I loved it! And as fall approached, we got a new enclosure for it, and he and I finishing putting it up (well, he assembled most of it even while being on oxygen). We made a great team.

Late October 2015

Robert asked me to comb his hair out again today after his shower. I didn't mind at all. God bless him. Anything requiring exertion, he got winded from. I prayed for him every morning and night.

November 2015

I had a serious talk with Robert and asked him to turn to his faith. I told him to ask God for help in this journey.

December 8, 2015

We got the call! Praise God. It was another cool night of watching hockey then relaxing after dinner. Robert was doing the dishes. I had nodded off, and Robert said, "Cherie, your phone is going off."

An Unknown Angel's Gift

I picked up my phone and saw our nurse coordinator's name appear. A beautiful bouquet of flowers appeared with her name (because that is the picture I have with her name)! I put the phone on speaker, and she said, "We have lungs for you, Robert." We looked at each other in utter shock but were joyful at the same time. We were making a couple of calls, and Robert was as cool as a cucumber. The nurse called back and asked, "How soon can you be here?" Robert said, "I am ready now." I, who I must say confidently have been prepared for years with bags packed for each season and a note on my corkboard of what to remember, was walking (frantically somewhat) through the house, feeling excited and knocking things over as I headed to get dressed and ready to roll. I turned on my television with the music channel I kept on during this holiday time, and what was playing was "Hark the Herald Angel Sing." Indeed, they do.

* * * * *

As I get chills while I am typing this, I know God had answered our prayers—finally. At long last, my husband, Robert, would get the lungs he deserved and feel so much better. The patient it told not to drive when they get that long-awaited call; however, Robert was cool, calm, and collected and drove us downtown to what would be another journey you will hear of in another chapter.

Thank you for having patience as I tried to easily explain the month-by-month medical trials we faced year after year in this chapter. I hope the next chapters find you enjoying the inspirational words of wisdom we heard, the quotes I read and wrote, the music that helped, the people that helped inspire us, and the many things we learned along the journey leading up to the call and the surgery that helped Robert learn to enjoy life again.

Cherie S. Blackwell

Chapter 3

Support

Who, Why, When, and the Support Groups

Helping someone is what life is all about.
—Willie Stargell

WHEN I THINK OF THE word *support*, I think of many meanings. It's not just who but why and when it is critical to not only an individual but also couples going through an illness together. You will have the people *who* genuinely care, *who* ask questions, *who* are there for you, *who* call you, *who* send you a card, and *who* not only ask how your ailing partner is but also how you are coping as well. You learn who genuinely cares and is not just an acquaintance in life. The acquaintances will ask the same questions that you have answered. Some are just being polite or just don't understand because they have never been through it, but you learn to avoid some people because when you are with your sick loved one and someone asks you questions, your loved one (in this case, my husband, who gets very winded from talking) will look to you to explain many situations. So I do to the best of my ability. You try to avoid added stressful situations because you don't want added stress, and this is because you have enough. I am not saying you should avoid a social situation. Use your judgement to decide if the situation is something you may need at that time in your life. If you are invited to something, you may have to politely decline if it is something you do not wish to be at in that particular stage of your loved one's illness. It is quite hard to explain unless you have been in this situation. I can only hope that by trying to explain different scenarios, you can gain insight from someone who has been through it.

As with any situation, as time goes on, you learn what works best for both of you in different social situations. The people, the timing, the location, etc.—many factors come into play when you are going somewhere. My husband would voice how stressful of a process it was for him when we were going somewhere because we had to plan for enough oxygen for that trip. A person who has an illness is already tired, so you have to think compassionately about this process and how they feel. I did just this when I would plan any kind of social outing for us. I made sure it was always a late lunch (between 2:00 p.m. and 4:00 p.m.)—when public places were less busy. It would be less stressful for us, and it would be less crowded, which meant less germs. We would also find that there were public places where people would stare when we go there at a later hour (when things were busier). This was stressful for me because I'd just want to say something like "Take a picture." But for the most part, as there has been more publicity for people of all ages and all conditions wearing oxygen, people have been more compassionate. Robert had a way of making social situations more comfortable also by telling a joke, or he'd explain to a younger child by undoing his oxygen cannula and simply saying, "See? It just helps me breathe easier" or placing the open cannula in my wine glass to aerate it.

As I delve into this chapter, you will find me mentioning many different people who played different roles in our lives and who are still there for us to this day. What a critical role they played throughout this whole process.

Support from family

Gran (my mom's mom). This is the first person I want to mention. She is my grandmother on my mother's side. She was always like a best friend to me. We talked frequently and shared everything.

An Unknown Angel's Gift

She was the type of person you could talk to with no judgement. She was a great judge of character, and she surely liked Robert from the get-go. She told me in the beginning of Rob and my relationship, "I know he is going to always take good care of you." I never doubted any words my grandmother told me throughout my whole life. Whenever I talked to her about anything, she always had the right thing to say whether they were just words of encouragement or advice. She always lent a kind ear and listened, and she was always fun to be around. You could have serious conversations or talk about relationships, friendships, food, pets, sports, comedy, television, travel, and even the times she had with my grandfather. She was one of the most interesting, kindest people I had the pleasure of having as my grandmother. When she learned of Robert's illness, she played such a huge part in our support system. She was always the type of person who would do anything for you, but in this case, I can recall many times she stayed with us. And she even went with us to appointments so I wouldn't have to wait alone while Robert went in for a test.

I remember one morning when we were driving downtown, and she said, "I have never been in the back seat, driving downtown at eighty miles per hour with toast in one hand and coffee in the other." It was funny at the time. Gran always had something funny to say. Gran always had a kind word to say about someone. Gran was always there for you. She offered the kind of support we really needed early on in accepting this whole process. She was genuine and kind, and she was someone *who* truly was there for us. She was always there for me my whole life, and to have her here briefly during this early phase in Robert's illness was a blessing. We lost her too young, and she is greatly missed. A true definition of a kindhearted soul was my gran. She was one of a kind. I am sure many of you have been lucky enough to have someone like this in your life. To those that do, you have been blessed. If you mentioned something, you had it a week later. God rest her soul. She was truly special and someone I wanted to be mentioned first in this book as she was really there early on for us before her passing.

She was an inspiration to all who knew her. She was an individual who was all heart, had a great sense of humor, and was always there for you.

And as I move forward, there are so many people to mention. I hope I remember them all.

Dad. My father has been someone who undeniably has been there constantly. When Robert lost his own father, he and my father became closer. I swear, they text and talk more than my father and me.

There has always been respect and understanding, which I recognized early on, between them, and they have a similar sense of humor. It's almost hard to put into words all the many ways my father has been there for us. He is kind, sincere, genuine, compassionate, and all around a person to be around. He attended almost all of our support meetings. When we talked, it wasn't all health related. There were jokes, car issues, family talk, and whatever just came to mind. He's just one of the easiest people to talk to and always has been, and he could make you laugh and feel comfortable at the drop of a dime.

An Unknown Angel's Gift

It's nice to be able to talk to a loved one when you are going through such a stressful situation. I truly believe my father "understood" exactly what we were going through. Having had his wife, my mom, become very ill early on in their marriage, I am sure he could relate to the stress and fear we were feeling. I could call him anytime, and he always knows what to say. When you have a spouse who has an illness and you have all these things you are trying to deal with and accept, it is nice to know you have someone you can call who can understand, listen without judgement, and help you through in so many ways. My dad had a way also of always complimenting me on my strength. This helped me immensely. When you have a spouse who is ill, people are quick to ask how the sick one is but not the spouse. In fact, when they do ask you, you are actually a little surprised and unsure of how to react as you are just trying to get through each day, not really thinking about your own emotions at the time, just trying to make it through each day and all the businesses of it all.

Dad and I were talking one afternoon in 2014, and he said, "You always think of others, so I want to do something for you and take you guys out for your birthday." I thought that was so kind. It really stood out as something kind and genuine, but I never expect anything different from my dad. He's got a heart of gold.

Claudia (stepmom). This woman has a strength I so admire. She says it like it is. She comes from a large family whose members all show a deep amount of respect for one another. I am so very grateful she is in our lives. So many times, she has had just the right thing to say at just the right moment. She is funny and straight to the point. Even as I get older and older, I have learned so much from her over the years. She has been a wonderful part of our support system along with dad; they are the ultimate power couple of strength and love that we need to look upon to give us that added strength/boost we need to carry on and defeat this illness, which takes on our day-by-day. I cannot really even put it into exact words. How do you thank two people who are always there to listen, talk, laugh, and spend time together with? We were taken away from the normal everyday monotony of what we were going through and had laughter and good times with two exceptional people who we have been blessed to call Dad and Mom. Both had frequented our support meetings year after year and learned about Robert's disease and the many different things that came along with it. Thank you, Claudia, for not only being my father's better half but also for being there for us, listening to us, and guiding us. You are truly an inspiration to all who know you.

Bill (brother). There are so many nice things I could say about my one and only brother, and I will. Early in our lives as toddlers and siblings, I am sure we got along as best we could. Growing up, we were faced with such tragedy: losing our mother at such a young age. I think that tragedy affected our relationship as youngsters/teens, meaning we did not get along. We did our own thing, and we tended to argue. Unfortunately, there was always tension between us. We never spoke of the tragedy that happened to us until later in our lives. We are survivors. We had wonderful people in our lives to help get us through. I can say that life had many challenges for us, but we made the right decisions and learned many lessons. We had guidance from both sets of grandparents and our father. When I think back, I realize that both of us grew up quickly, leaving our childhood behind and coping every day as best we could. I remember having so many different emotions, being angry at my brother and family. I realize we may not have been close in our younger lives, but we are now. And it means everything.

As we struggled through our lives, I watched him mature and become a great man, learned of his likes and dislikes. I am sure he had much anger as well. I am sure we were not as angry at each other as we were at losing our mother and the unfairness of it.

I will only say this about the day I was told my mother had passed: I will never forget hearing my brother crying in his room, seeing the hurt on my father's face, and the feeling of how long each day had passed as kids. I clung to taking care of the house, cooking, baking, and making sure he and Dad seemed okay. As long as everyone else was okay, I was okay. As long as my surroundings were okay, I was okay. I took care of the house, and that helped me cope each day. I have very few memories, and the story of my life would be another book. And we are focusing on the last ten years of my life, not the first ten.

I learned in my twenties through a wonderful counselor all the many emotions I never dealt with and why I felt the way I did. As an adult, I understand why I act and react the way I do to everything. I am grateful I was able to speak with a professional to sort it all out. Now let me tell you all the nice things about my brother.

Now that I am much older, I am so grateful for my brother. I realize what a wonderful person he turned out to be. He is kind, sincere, funny, bright, hardworking, ambitious, and great to talk to. I have never respected a father more than when watching him with and supporting his kids, and now as a grandfather, he's passing the same morals on to them. He is great around his friends and family, and it has been wonderful to see him develop a better relationship with our father. As a brother-in-law to Robert, it's really cool also. He and Robert talk with and text each other as well, and it means so much to have a supportive, loving brother who is there for us. Thank you, Bill, for being a brother we respect and love.

Joan (Bill's wife and our sister-in-law). I met Joan thirty years ago, and I knew back then we would always be friends. We had similar likes, dislikes, and family values. She is the best thing that ever happened to my brother. She is a great mother and grandmother. Joan is someone you can sit and talk to for hours on the phone or in person. She was a great part of my support system and continues to be a great friend. I am so glad she is a part of our family.

Stephanie and Scott and their spouses *(our niece and nephew and my brother's two kids).* Two wonderful, inspirational, supportive young adults in this journey of ours. Thank you!

Michelle and Don M. (Joan's sister and husband). Two very caring, genuine people who are so supportive in our journey. Thank you!

An Unknown Angel's Gift

Michael (Robert's brother). Mike, one of Rob's three brothers, closest in age to him, played the biggest part in his support system other than my dad. Mike has always been there for Robert. Mike is someone who is genuine, kind, and funny. He and Robert are a lot alike, and when I see them together, I can see why they have always been close. They both remind me of their father. They have a connection, a common ground, a common bond. It makes me very happy to know Robert always had his support. Mike always called Robert before and after the transplant, and he was there the whole night of his surgery and throughout the post-op journey. Robert is very lucky to have Mike as a brother. Their sense of humor together was a huge help in Robert's journey. Thanks, Mike, for being you!

Lori (our sister-in-law and Michael's wife). Lori is an absolute gem. She is Mike's better half and confidant. She is extremely intelligent, thoughtful, and sincere. We have had many dinners together, the four of us, having fun outside of this medical phenomenon Robert and I had to deal with. She was very helpful/knowledgeable in this journey. I cannot even explain all the times she has helped us. Thanks, Lori, for being so kind, and we are so grateful for you.

An Unknown Angel's Gift

Ron and his wife, Nancy (Loris' father, who had transplant also, and his wife, Nancy, his support). There are not enough words to describe what an incredible man Ron was. Robert knew Ron when he also was on oxygen for a debilitating lung disease. He had his transplant and was a mentor to both of us. Ron had a warm smile and an even warmer soul. He was always smiling. He was always telling a good story. He was always there to lend a helping hand. We learned so much from Ron, and he guided us in many ways in our journey with Robert's disease. I remember that early on (October 2008), he gave us many videos, books, and literature so we could learn more about what we were about to embark on. He was easy to talk to. He attended all the lung transplant support meetings even after he had his surgery. He came for many years, and that taught us early on how important support is. And he mentored others as they embarked on a scary journey no matter what their age or condition might be. Ron's wife, Nancy, was also right there by his side at the meetings and was there for any kind of support needed. She's a wonderful lady I learned a lot from. We will be forever grateful to have had them in our lives. We lost Ron too soon, but we still continue to brag about him and just how wonderful he was. I am sure he was in the operating room as one of the many guardian angels watching over Robert with lots of added strength and insight!

Jeff (Robert's oldest brother). Jeff is an inspiration to all who know him. He has this amazing personality. He is one of the most interesting and knowledgeable people I have ever met. Also, he's genuine. He has been to our home many times and to the hospital. He always made sure to keep in touch with Rob before, during, and after his transplant. I am so grateful for this man—Robert's oldest brother—being in our lives.

Tim (Robert's youngest brother). Tim is not one to show his emotions. Tim has always been there for us to help with anything we need around the house. On the day of Robert's surgery, Tim was there for most of day, sitting in the hospital room. I could see the concern on his face. He was very interested in and wanted to know the status of his brother. I am glad he was able to come and see Robert during his hospital stay.

Jill (Robert's sister). There are not enough words to describe this wonderful lady; she's always loving and supportive. She is like the sister I never had. We have always had a connection. She is the type of person you can talk to about anything with no judgement or harshness, just support. Robert is so lucky to have such a wonderful sister. She also has always called (as she lives out of state) before, during, and after Robert's transplant and always sent nice cards, or she had something uplifting to say to lift our spirits. God bless her. She is a gem. Her husband, Kirk, is also a phenomenal person with his great sense of humor and also huge amount of support. I am so glad he is Jill's husband and family.

Mike Jr., Collin, and Kristyn (Robert's nephews and niece in Michigan). I could go on and on about these outstanding nephews and niece. Each of them have a sense of care for their uncle Robert and a sense of humor. There is a closeness there that there are no words for, and I am also very grateful for them. Before, during, and after the surgery, they made sure to know the status of their uncle Rob.

Niece Kelsey—A wonderful person with a wonderful soul.

Dawn (Robert's youngest brother's [Tim] ex-wife). Dawn is one of the most bighearted, intelligent women I have ever met. She is one of my best friends. She was always there for us to lend a kind word or offer help in any way that was needed. I can never thank her enough for the many times her words helped me. Her support will never be forgotten, always treasured.

Aunt Judy. I can see why my mother and Aunt Judy (my dads' sister) were so close. She is another extremely intelligent person who's easy to talk to about anything. I remember one day in particular. I was having a rough day at the hospital, and I called her. God always knew who I needed to call me.

Her words of inspiration and encouragement got me through the toughest of times when I thought I could not do it. She said things from experience, knowledge, and love. I will be forever grateful I was able to speak with her on that one particular day in the hospital.

Support from friends

Jamey and Angela (friends) (Jamey listed at U of M, and Angela is his wife). I think back to years ago when Robert mentioned Jamey, a guy he met while working out in a pulmonary rehab center. They were both on oxygen, and both began to talk, seeing they had a huge common interest other than their illness: cars. As time went on, we also met his wife Angela and their two children—Ashley and Jacob. It is really nice to have friends that you can share a common bond as scary as this with. We quickly realized we did have the support of one another and got to know one another through many a car show and many a dinner.

I am so grateful for the friendship we have all gained in this journey. From a spouse's perspective, it has been nice to be able to know I am not the only one going through it. We know how afraid we were that first year, and I could sense a similar fear in them. They had been attending their U of M meetings, and we our Henry Ford Support meetings as well. We attended their meetings, and they attended ours. We have all learned so much in this journey. Even while Robert was in the hospital, they came to visit. Jamey checked on Robert daily, came to visit, and asked if we needed anything. The friendship we have gained with them is immeasurable. They are two very unique, giving, smart, supportive friends. I am so grateful we all came across one another's paths. Everything happens for a reason. God believed we all needed one another, so he placed us in one another's paths. There have been many laughs, much learning, guidance, and direction from one another. People who have been through thick and thin together as long as us and have been there before, during, and after—these are the kinds of people you want in your life. They mean the world to us.

Al and Diane (friends Robert grew up with). What I love most about Al and Diane is the ability we all have to laugh together. When we were around them, I forgot all our stresses of Robert's illness. We have had many a talk, many a BBQ, and a strong bond of friendship. Robert has been lucky enough to have their friendship for nearly his whole life, and I am lucky to know and have them as friends as well. I remember during Robert's transplantation hospital stay the long phone conversation we had with them. It was so genuine and heartfelt. They are the type of people you thank God for every day. The laughter, the love, the friendship… Thank you, Al and Diane, for being you and for your undeniable kindness, support, and unending laughter. We love you!

Alane (a friend of mine for twenty-plus years). Here is someone who knows the true meaning of friendship. She is always there to listen and communicate like a friend should. It's so nice to be able to laugh a lot with a true friend. A friend is someone who listens, trusts, and communicates and is always there for you. Thank you, Alane, for always picking up when I called and for all the wonderful lunches we shared.

Lene (a friend of mine for twenty-plus years). Lene is like the sister I never had. We're both Aquarians, both with many of the same views and both driven to get what we want out of life. She is inspiring and fun, and she's a great friend who has also always been there for me.

Debbie (a friend of mine for thirty-plus years). Debbie is the funniest person I know. We could talk or shop for hours together. It's so nice to share a mojito or wine and chitchat with a true friend, who I am so lucky to have. Thanks, Debbie, for always being there when I needed a friend to cheer me up when I was so scared of the unexpected!

Shelly (a friend of mine for thirty-plus years). Shelly and I have an unspoken friendship—meaning, we may not talk often, but that special friendship has always been there. She says it like it is and also can make you laugh. I'm so glad to have another friend who is just a text away.

Roberta (a coworker of mine). Roberta will forever be in my heart. She had been a true friend from the time I started at my place of employment. We could talk about anything. A day never passed where she did not ask about Robert, and we always had our 5-o'clock pow-wow at the end of our days and discussed everything from family and friends to what was for dinner to a joke to make us laugh together. She passed too young from an illness and will forever be missed, but I'm so grateful to have known her.

Gwen (a coworker [biller] of mine). Gwen really helped me with insurance questions early on and throughout the process. I do not think I could have made it without her expertise and knowledge of insurance. I cannot even count the times I went to her with insurance questions and she made it all make sense to me. She also made me laugh and gave me general guidance—words of wisdom I needed to hear—at just the right time. She made a crazy day I didn't understand make sense. Because of her, I had the answers I needed to cope.

Pat R and Pat D (coworkers of mine). These are my two work moms and great friends. Both are genuine and sincere. Both make me laugh. Both give me insight. Both have children of their own and so many life circumstances. They always put things into perspective for me, and to this day, they are still two really great friends. I am so thankful to have them both in my life.

Diane (a coworker of mine). What a beautiful soul. Her smile is infectious, and her character is inspiring. She gave me a gift one year with the word *hope* inscribed on it—a candle holder. It was just beautiful. The following poem was enclosed:

> Hope
> Hope is like a candle flame.
> It flickers now and then,
> Sometimes we all need help to see,
> the strength that lies within.
> For life's not always easy,
> We're bound to have some sorrow,
> But hope can keep us going,
> for a better day tomorrow.
> So when you light this candle, and the flame is
>   burning bright,
> May the Angels bring you hope,
> And turn the darkness into light.

Rebeca (a coworker of mine). Rebeca became another great friend of mine. I have a huge amount of respect for her. She is knowledgeable and family oriented, and she is my favorite person to share an ice cream with. She also is a great listener and kind, and she has helped me in so many ways. I admire her patience, understanding, and points of view.

Bev M. A true friend and coworker who is an inspiration to talk to. Her smile lights up a room, and her personality is a gift. She always helps me with our talks.

An Unknown Angel's Gift

Christy (a coworker of mine). Christy has also become a great friend of mine. From the start, we connected, and she has always been a great listener. We can talk television, military, family, or home remodeling. Whatever the subject is, it's always interesting, and I am so grateful to have someone like her to know and work with. She has a great work ethic and takes pride in her work like me, and I have a huge amount of respect for her. I am so glad I have had the pleasure to get to know her.

JoAnn S. (a former coworker of mine, now retired). If you need to laugh or need it to be told like it is, just get with JoAnn. She is another incredibly vibrant person I have had the pleasure of knowing who always listened throughout this whole process. Thanks, JoAnn, for always putting a smile on my face!

Margaret and Joe (one of Robert's first pulmonary therapists and her husband). Margaret invited us to her home many times before and after Robert's transplant. What a great couple. They inspire anyone. We enjoy spending time with them. They have a beautiful home on a lake. They are knowledgeable, and I am so glad they are in our lives.

Tom and Debbie. When I think of these two, I think of two people that we laugh with the hardest. Wonderful, caring, supportive, great people to be around. Years of friendship that stand the test of time. So very grateful for them and the laughter and encouragement they have given us over the years and continue to. Thanks, Tom and Debbie, for being you! As longtime friends of Robert from work, we all connected and became the greatest of friends via car shows, dinners, parties, and gatherings.

John and Mary. Here is a friend Robert grew up with who became listed for a double-lung transplant. I am happy to say he reached out to us, and we helped to mentor him and his wife through the difficult processes and what to expect! Throughout this experience, we have become great friends who confide in and trust one another. John got his transplant, and Robert has helped him every step of the way. And we helped Mary through the bumps along the road and the ups and downs of things that can come about with a transplant as far as complications. It's a very emotional journey, and we have all helped one another and laughed together every chance we get! We are grateful for you both in our lives.

Pete and Stephanie. Longtime friends of Robert from the place of employment he retired from. Spent much time together at car shows and also became great friends. Two supportive people with the biggest hearts who would do anything for you. Thank you to both of you!

Sharon (BCBS case management nurse). I talked to Sharon month after month, year after year. This had to be done to make sure Blue Cross Blue Shield was kept in the loop and would therefore pay their portion! I will say that I highly recommend keeping in touch with your insurance case management person. They are educated nurses who are very compassionate and can answer any question you have, and they even bring up things you never would have thought of. So kudos to insurance companies for making sure their nurses keep up with the scoop on the patient's health condition.

Lauri and Patti (nurse coordinators). They were the first two nurse coordinators we had, and they were iconic and awesome! I am so glad these two nurses were the first two coordinators that we had the pleasure of knowing. It never felt like "Oh my god, another doctor visit!" These two were the most personable people we ever had the pleasure of knowing. They made our visits fun. In the first year Robert was listed, they put him through what is called a fast track of appointments: you name it, you get tested for it.

The hospital has seventeen floors. We saw every one of them including the floors of other buildings nearby as well. They have moved on to other facilities. We keep in touch to this day, over ten years later, and I am so grateful for this. Talk about two people who stepped into the perfect career. Thank you for making us feel at ease at every appointment. Thank you for coming to visit Robert at the hospital after his transplant even many years after you had left the facility. You took time out of your busy day to come see us. Since they had moved on, we have had numerous nurse coordinators, and all have done a fabulous job. We are grateful to each and every one of them.

An Unknown Angel's Gift

Michael B. (nurse and physician's assistant at Henry Ford). This gentleman was someone we met early on in the transplant process. Mike has a way of uplifting, educating, and inspiring you and making you feel at ease. He is a very interesting person. His faith draws you to him as well. I am so grateful Mike was there for us early in the process at the hospital. He educated us in so many ways. To this day, we keep in touch. He came to visit Robert also after his transplant many years after he left the facility. It goes to show you the type of character this person has. He came to visit and sat with us for hours, uplifting us and making us feel so much better. Thank you, Mike. You are a true hero in our eyes!

Kelly B. Thank you for being you and being with us throughout this incredible journey as we attend the lung transplant support-group meetings. You are a true gem to all who know you. Robert really enjoyed the heart-to-heart talk you both had after his transplant.

Bill M. A Life Flight coordinator we had the pleasure of getting to know year after year at the transplant support meetings. He was compassionate and educated us so much during the whole process and is such an inspiration!

Support group acquaintances in the past, present, and future. We have over ten years of acquaintances. Where do I begin? Early on, I offered to help keep all attendees and staff in the loop regarding the support meetings and have stayed involved ever since. You learn so much before and after the process, especially during the waiting process. Throughout this part, I may not mention them by name, but I will tell you what we gained from them at a particular meeting. I hope you find this helpful as you read, and I hope that if you ever come across a situation where you may need additional support from someone other than family and friends—from someone who is going through the exact same process, you will not think twice about how helpful it is to just sit and listen to someone else's story and realize, *Wow, I am not in this alone. There are many, many others who are going through the same thing, and their spouses and other loved ones are experiencing the same doubts, fears, hopes and dreams!*

I will discuss some of the many support meetings after I pay tribute to the doctors that really stood out and continue to stand out.

Be sensitive to one another's needs and the ever-changing stages of the illness process.

The doctors

Dr. A. This doctor was very impressive. In 2008, she made us as well as the family feel very comfortable in a stressful situation. We were educated and offered hope with Robert's condition. We are so grateful to this day for Dr. A's devotion, understanding, and knowledge!

Dr. S. Dr. S is also so amazing, knowledgeable, and straightforward. She tells you just what you need to hear in simple, easy-to-understand terms. We are also very grateful for her continued support, understanding, and interesting clinic visits and suggestions to keep Robert on the right track.

Dr. K. What a super cool, enthusiastic doctor who makes you feel at ease from the get-go. We were very sad to see her go; however, everyone must follow where life may lead them.

Dr. B. Early on, this was the only doctor we did not like. However, after time, he became quite likable, and we enjoyed the time we were able to see him. He also moved out of state to pursue other things.

Fellows and nurse practitioners. I can't say enough good things about the fellows who come into the exam room before the doctor and make you feel comfortable or at ease with the many questions they must ask!

The many, many lung transplant support meetings

Fall to winter 2008. I remember one of the very first meetings we attended and how emotional it made me feel. I am a very sensitive person anyhow, and these meetings really hit home on how a medical condition affects the spouse, family members, and friends. We had a very close acquaintance who had heart issues that we also went to visit in the ICU. This was very difficult and a real eye-opener to what we may go through in the future. I remember thinking at that moment, *Will I see my husband in a bed, tubed, often?* I remember meeting a Gift of Life coordinator early on also and getting educated on Robert giving future talks about his condition. Moving right along, there was so much information to take in, so many emotions, and so much to learn. It can all feel overwhelming, but every person you hear something from will help you in your journey.

Spring to summer 2009. There were numerous small open discussions that went extremely well.

2013. We learned some great, helpful tips for transplant patients I would like to share. Be proactive! If you are not feeling quite right, don't ignore the symptoms or wait until you are really sick to take action. Remember, this is team sport, and you have an incredible team that is only a phone call away. Don't hesitate to call your UMHS Transplant Center nurse (Heidi, Roz, Cathy, etc.) for advice and directions. They know the special needs of lung transplant patients and your special needs, and they draw on the knowledge base of the transplant team. If it is nothing to worry about, they will happily tell you so. They can arrange scripts as needed and make adjustments to your meds if needed. Or they can provide direction for your treatment. It is much easier to do an ounce of prevention at the source than to cure a complicated mix of things later.

Family physicians and local hospitals are important caregivers but generally have little awareness of the special needs of lung transplant patients. Even with the best intentions, they may prescribe something that could be counterproductive, preclude transplantation, or create other major problems for the immunosuppressed. Your physician can call UM for information and advice on your special needs. Your nurse contact can provide information when contact is needed.

If you need care away from the area, go to a transplant center, ideally one that serves lung transplant patients. But any transplant center will at least be tuned in to the special needs of those who are immunosuppressed or waiting for a transplant. And don't hesitate to have a physician call your pulmonologist at UMHS to consult on your treatment. If the physician won't consult, find another. That one likely doesn't know or care about what he doesn't know, and that is dangerous to you.

If you need to go to an emergency clinic, before all else, tell them you are a lung transplant patient (whether pre- or posttransplant). They can hopefully isolate you or separate you from all the sick people.

If you are in a crowd or around people who may be sick, wear a mask. It provides a little direct protection, but its best value is that most people think you "have something" and try to stay away from you, which is exactly what you want.

Use hand sanitizer often and keep some handy to offer those friendly folks who may inadvertently share germs you should avoid.

Stay active and engaged. Continue doing the stuff you love to do to the extent you can. Just take common-sense precautions, as noted above. It is important for your emotional health as well as physical health. Pulmonary rehab is especially helpful pre- and post-transplant. The social benefits are as important as the physical. Also, carry these at all times:

- doctor's, nurses', and the emergency transplant team's number
- medication list

Remember to do these as well:

- Call them before taking anything; no herbal supplements (they can cause dangerous drug interactions)
- Call them on anything (e.g., toothache, travel, etc.)
- Pick two people-patient advocates
- The pre-clinic appointment's *mandatory*, and so are the *post-clinic* appointments. You *must go*.

An Unknown Angel's Gift

The years 2010–2014 were a complete blur as far as meetings were concerned, but we attended every month and found them all heartwarming.

July 2014. This was a tremendous meeting that I remember quite well. There was a gentleman we got to know quite well who had been with us throughout the whole process (this meeting was on stress management and really hit me hard). I cried a lot. We learned someone we cared for deeply was leaving Henry Ford to move forward elsewhere in his career. He said this was not goodbye. He invited us to his church. I believe God worked through him to send us a message. What a tremendous spirit he has. He always made us feel important. I have prayed often throughout this experience that Robert's faith would be renewed or restored and that he continues to have faith.

December 2014. Robert signed up for a study after a support meeting today. Around 252 people in the US were in it. We were informed it might offer him a bigger opportunity for another lung offer. At this meeting, we met a couple where the gentleman had just his transplant two months prior, and they both offered us much insight and hope. I am grateful we got to meet them.

I recall everyone mentioning, "God, it's in your hands today." I love the messages of faith at the support group meetings. It reinstills the fact that you must have faith. I believe God will carry us throughout the journey. He already is!

2015–2017. As I truly reflect on these meetings, I realize how much I learned from others during this journey.

Early on, I offered to take on the responsibility of taking the attendees' information, which would allow me to email them each month and let them know the location, time, and speakers or any other relevant information that might be helpful to them. I don't know if this was just something I felt I needed to do, if God sent me this message to try and help others more, or if it was just my kind nature wanting to help in this trying time when we just were so hungry to learn. The staff were nothing but courteous and have allowed me to do this to this day. I enjoy it. I enjoy not only seeing the staff each month, but also, Robert and I have learned so much and have met so many others in the same boat.

I can honestly say that I truly learned that seeing another person (patient and spouse) in the same boat and hearing their stories will help you. You share similar fears. You share things that have helped you in the journey. I believe that each meeting gives you an answer to something you need an answer to.

After nearly ten years, there are too many people during these meetings to name that helped us in this journey, and hopefully, we helped them also. I remember going to the support group while Robert was in the hospital and how scared I was. I don't know if it was exhaustion or the fear breaking down while telling all these wonderful souls we finally got "the call"—the gift that we waited so long for. My father was with me every step of the way. We went, and I told them all how great Robert had been doing and how we finally received the gift. And it was in the month of December, which made it the best Christmas gift ever. The hardest part was knowing someone lost a loved one and how their holiday would be so sad but that we would be celebrating because we received a gift.

Robert and I continue to go to the support groups even after he received the gift. We realize that you must give back to those waiting, who are as scared as we were that first time we walked into a support meeting, not knowing what to expect.

I would like to pay tribute to all those we have met during the wait, the ones we have talked to after the surgery while in the hospital who received their gift also during the holidays, and the ones we continue to meet, to whom we try to give back and help as the many unselfish others did by coming after their surgeries to offer hope.

I want to thank the staff at the hospital. Without them, nothing would be possible in this journey.

I want to thank my husband for being my inspiration as we go to these meetings, where I listen to him talk and inspire others.

Lastly, thank you to all I mentioned in this chapter. Without your support, I don't think I could have made it through what I thought was a never-ending journey of fear and a roller coaster of emotions. Your support system truly is made up of the people in your life who are there for you through thick and thin, not just the good times.

I will close with this verse from Proverbs 14:21: "Blessed is he who is kind to the needy."

Chapter 4

Gift of Life

Stories along Rob's Incredible Journey

What oxygen is to the lungs, such is hope to the meaning of life.
—Emil Brunner

September 2012

A WOMAN NAMED BETSY WHO WAS affiliated with Gift of Life reached out to us and wanted Robert to do a video with many others waiting for transplant. Robert wanted to do this near the Joe Louis Arena, where we enjoyed many hockey games together. We drove downtown on a cool fall day (the twenty-seventh, to be exact), and there was a camera crew and a script for Robert to read. It was exhilarating to see him speak so confidently about a disease that had struck him, preventing him from enjoying so much. As he stated in the video, "Only a lung transplant will save my life."

I remember when the video came out, and it was distinctly directed to residents of Wayne County as there was a dire need for people to sign up from Wayne County. So appropriately did they name the segment "Waiting to Live." I remember the others that played roles in the video: a gentleman waiting for a liver, two women waiting for kidneys, and a young girl waiting for a heart. All of these people spoke in front of different Detroit venues, and it was heartwarming to see their segment but also scary to see their struggle. As I understand it, many of those in the video lost their lives, unfortunately, waiting…with one still waiting. God bless them for sharing with others to promote organ donation and show the reality of the wait and fear.

April 2013

It had been many years already into this journey, and I had reflected much about all of the situations and people that have crossed out path, all of them put there for a reason. Of course, it goes without saying that Ron was a person who really educated us on the Gift of Life, its process, and the people that make it all work. God bless him and the wonderful impact he had on us during this journey.

Again, a specific person I must mention is Betsy from Gift of Life. She reached out to us first in April 2013 again and wanted Robert to speak at a Gift of Life event symposium with over four hundred doctors and staff present.

Rob wanted me to ask Betsy why she would want him to speak, so I did. And she said that he was a real person and that people would want a heartfelt perspective of someone waiting. What an honor; they had numerous speakers that were pre- and post-transplant, many like Robert, who was still waiting for that gift of life. I was filled with a tremendous amount of pride once again as I stood and watched my husband explain this long battle he has been through and express his feelings to all these strangers. He has always had a gift of expressing himself to others, but to speak in front of all of these people took a lot of courage and strength, which he exudes every day.

Thank you, Betsy, for reaching out and asking Robert to do this. He not only touched me but many others as well, especially the medical staff, so they would be able to see an emotional point of view from a patient. And that he did—a beautiful touching perspective.

April was also a month with a Gift of Life symposium at a hospital in Detroit where donor families are honored. There was such a huge amount of love and support everywhere. Dad and Claudia were in attendance that day also. It was a very emotional presentation.

Again, April was also momentous in the time spent with Robert's oldest brother Jeff and his roommate Jon, who I taught how to dance because his daughter's wedding was approaching. We also had a wonderful dinner with Robert's other brother Mike and his wife, Lori, as well as close friends on a different day—Alan and Diane. These types of get-togethers with friends and family are what helped us keep our sanity throughout this whole process.

2012 to 2015

The next three events between 2012 and 2015 were also very significant memories we created:

- Event in Ann Arbor honoring transplant patients with media. Once again, we are asked to attend. It was a very emotional experience.
- Event in Lansing where Robert and I marched with pre- and posttransplant patients and donor families. Lori (our sister-in-law) and her dad, Ron, both marched also. Both were also tissue/organ recipients. Dad and Claudia were present also as well as Robert's brother Mike.
- Event in Downtown Detroit where Robert and I marched with pre- and posttransplant patients and their families again. It was a very wonderful experience. Jamey, Robert's transplant friend who was going along the journey, also marched with us this day. Both of them were still waiting for the gift!

From 2008 through 2015, there were numerous talks we were lucky enough to attend with Gift of Life workers; and from each and every story shared, we learned something new. You would not go through this whole process without learning something from so many volunteers and people who have lost loved ones and become volunteers for Gift of Life. Their stories touch us so deeply.

May 2014

I watched an organ donation special, which is something that's becoming more and more prevalent. It was called "Living and Nonliving." I very interesting and enlightening special on organ donation!

* * * * *

Posttransplant, we still attend many Gift of Life talks. Their speakers are inspiring, and we are so glad to be volunteers. We have completed the paperwork required. We try to share our story with many and help them understand organ donation. We volunteered at a symposium in 2017 where we wrote and handed out name tags for donor families attending a ceremony to honor the donor families. What an emotional experience. We talked with two people working with us at the table who had lost loved ones and also received organs, like Robert. At the conclusion of the ceremony, where many who received organs or tissue spoke, there were many of us asked to bring up a poster board we had made that said thank you and hold it up in the front of the room while facing the families who had lost loved ones whose organs were donated. During this process, a young girl who received a heart was singing and playing the harp. I cried throughout the whole song. It was beautiful, and like I said earlier in the descriptions of these events, it is very touching/moving to be a part of all of this.

I am so grateful every day that we have a chance to be educated through these Gift of Life events, many at Henry Ford and the U of M Hospital. And we have met so many wonderful people pre- and posttransplant as well as many donor families who have lost loved ones, their organs saving so many lives.

There's a common myth that's heard while at attendance at many of the meetings and also heard through a family member: when you go into a hospital and the doctors and staff know you are an organ donor, they will not work their hardest to save your life. Fact: This is not true. Doctors take an oath to, by all means possible, save your life. If there are any questions about things heard regarding organ donation, contact someone at Gift of Life directly if you are uncertain of an answer, or you may visit the website: giftoflife.org.

Of note, I must not close this chapter without also mentioning another wonderful soul we have met—Kim. Thank you for guiding us in the process and helping us become more educated.

As it stands today, where I am in the process of this book, Robert and I have sent the third letter to the donor family of Robert's donor, and we hope to meet the family very soon. If it is meant to be, it will be. If or when this does happen, it will be discussed later in the book.

Henry Ford and Gift of Life have mentioned media in this process. We will leave that up to the donor family as to how, when, and where they wish to meet if that day comes.

Thank you, donor. Thank you, Gift of Life—an unbelievable group of people doing an amazing job and just another example of an organization that works extremely hard to do what they do.

This is a short, sweet chapter, but it's one that holds so much meaning to our gratefulness to Gift of Life and all the moments we treasure and will continue to make.

This quote fits the closing of this chapter and those thinking on those waiting for the ultimate gift:

You will receive a high prize or award soon.

Anyone waiting knows that if they receive the gift of life, it is the ultimate reward, because all the challenges a patient and their support system face throughout their journey their ultimate reward is receiving that gift and doing everything they can to show their appreciation for that gift because it is the *gift of life*.

Here are some very heartwarming photos from different Gift of Life events we attended and were a part of:

August 2012, Detroit, Michigan.
Shooting video for "Waiting to Live."

August 2012, Detroit, Michigan.
Continued footage of the "Waiting to Live" video.

August 2012, Detroit, Michigan.
It's a wrap—"Waiting to Live" Wayne County video at Joe Louis Arena.

September 2012, Ann Arbor, Michigan.

September 2013, Lansing, Michigan.

September 2013, Lansing, Michigan.

September 2013, Lansing, Michigan.

September 2013, Lansing, Michigan.

September 2013, Lansing, Michigan.

September 2013, Lansing, Michigan.

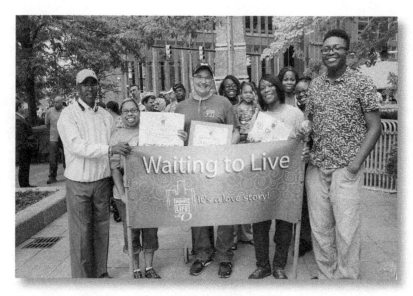

September 2016, Detroit, Michigan.

September 2016, Detroit, Michigan.

An Unknown Angel's Gift

September 2016, Detroit, Michigan.

September 2016, Detroit, Michigan.

September 2016, Detroit, Michigan.

September 2016, Detroit, Michigan.

Gift of Life ad.

Organ donation picture.

Cherie S. Blackwell

(excerpt from the poem)
To Remember Me

Give my sight to the man who has never seen a sunrise, a baby's face, or love in the eyes of a woman.

Give my heart to a person whose own heart has caused nothing but endless days of pain.

Give my blood to the teenager who was pulled from the wreckage of his car, so that he might live to see his grandchildren play.

Give my kidneys to one who depends on a machine to exist from week to week.

Take my bones, every muscle, every fiber and nerve in my body and find a way to make a crippled child walk.

Explore every corner of my brain. Take my cells, if necessary, and let them grow so that, someday, a speechless boy will shout at the crack of a bat and a deaf girl will hear the sound of rain against her window.

Burn what is left of me and scatter the ashes to the winds to help the flowers grow.

If you must bury something, let it be my faults, my weaknesses and all prejudice against my fellow man.

Give my sins to the devil.

Give my soul to God.

If, by chance, you wish to remember me, do it with a kind deed or word to someone who needs you.

If you do all I have asked, I will live forever.

Poem shared at most events.

An Unknown Angel's Gift

Butterflies—always a beautiful sign of life.

Gift of Life "Hope: Donate Life" saying.

The Donate Life flag hung at numerous events.

Thank you for allowing me to share these wonderful pictures of events dear to our hearts.

Here is a pic of Robert and me volunteering at a Gift of Life table, getting the word out about the importance of organ donation:

Chapter 5

Life's Journey

Adjustments...with Everything and outside of the Lung Issues

The past will eat you alive, but the future will save you.
— Ben, *Survivor* winner

As I sit here, I reflect on so much. The minutes and days go by so very fast but not when you're waiting for your loved one to get better.

I remember sitting in the hospital lobby one night while my husband was still in the ICU. I was thinking of all the titles of the chapters I would use for this book. This one is particularly difficult because how do you explain adjusting to something that is never expected? So many thoughts go racing through your mind at so many times. I remember all these moments quite vividly; I would walk away from that hospital room and from watching Robert fight hard to get better and better. I would go to the chapel or find myself in that hospital lobby, staring at the large decorated Christmas tree and all the red poinsettias around it, thinking, *How am I going to adjust to this?* I would think of this lifesaving gift my husband received and the heartache of the donor's family as I sat in that hospital lobby.

Every day is a new, scary experience and a learning experience. To adjust to something, I would just pray I would make it through. Back then, every time I would have those moments where I practically felt like running, I would stop by that lobby and call a family member or friend. And for that brief moment, I felt sane.

I believe I am a very strong person and try to be the rock for all around me, especially my husband, who I was watching day by day work so hard at everything expected of him to recover. And here I was, making sure I was adjusting to all that came with it.

Now let me talk about the early adjustments in this process.

First and foremost, as mentioned in the first chapter, we need *acceptance.* But do you ever accept the inevitable? The patient, spouse, family, and friends must accept and support. I believe the person who finds it the hardest to accept is the patient. Can you imagine being told by a doctor about your illness, what to expect, and what you must to do survive? How do I explain all the emotions a patient experiences? I am telling you this from the spouse's eyes.

They say God only gives you as much as you can handle. Every person's strength is tested with every situation, and acceptance is one of the most important characteristics a patient faces. Face this illness with your spouse head-on, be compliant, and hope that you live through it, all the while watching, just being supportive. As the spouse, you may be afraid to voice your fears as it is stressful enough for the patient to accept and do what they need to do to feel well enough to cope each day. You have to just hope for the best and be supportive. We found through many people we met at support meetings that marriages end because the spouse cannot handle it. Here is what I must say: When you took your vows, it was for better or worse, right? Stand by your spouse and support them every step of their journey.

The next point is about *your schedules.* Now, you must understand that any illness may take you down that road of the patient (your spouse) needing to retire or stop working because their profession will not allow oxygen or the many appointments and treatments that may be needed. So whatever you are used to is going to *completely* change. They will be home more often. They will be facing all their emotions squarely in front of you. You have to be patient, which may not easy. *Everything* you were used to is going to change. All the things the patient enjoys, they will slowly not be able to do. They will be very angry and emotional, and so will you. I can honestly say I was not angry; I was compassionate. I would think that if the shoe were on the other foot, I would hope they would be compassionate also. Not only are their careers ending, but the things they enjoy at home are changing. And this is making them feel helpless. All you can do as the spouse is be encouraging and supportive. Sure, you will miss all the extra things they do for you, but you hope and pray that one day, they will be able to do it again at an even better pace.

The next point is this: *welcome to a life of numerous doctor appointments and medical bills*! This is your life now. As the spouse, you will want to take as much stress off your spouse as possible. If you're like me, you will take over keeping up with these things because they are trying hard enough to accept and cope, and the added stress of making appointments and following up on medical bills, I feel, could send them off the deep end. In our situation, we were fortunate because I have a medical background and medical insurance knowledge, and I know what to ask.

The next point is this: *get a hold of the medical supply store.* In our particular situation, we needed many medical supplies delivered, and they were not cheap. There are so many things to keep up with that it will make your head spin. If you do not have high blood pressure or are fairly carefree or happy-go-lucky, the things I have discussed thus far will slowly make you feel like you are losing your mind. So proceed to get a hold of the medical supply store. Here are the things you will need on a constant basis: First is an oxygen concentrator (which we had fun deciding which room to place it in; we went through four different rooms before we—specifically Robert—decided on the basement with a long extended version of an oxygen cord running up through the ceiling because that concentrator machine was so damn loud that it sounded like a consistent freight train running through the home… and guess what? Adjust to it because it is your life now). Then you have all the big green oxygen tanks, which you need to store because you have to fill them on the concentrator if you want to go anywhere. And you have the big cart tank and regulator, your portable O_2 unit and charger, and any other miscellaneous supplies that go with it. And don't forget the maintenance this thing will need to keep it working properly. And if you have a power outage, better make damn sure you have tanks full to last for hours or a generator.

And when you call with questions, do you have someone who cares, or is that person just going through the motions? And then there is the time they want you to come to their store directly to pick up something. When you get there, take a number. Don't be in a hurry. Many there are in the same boat or need similar supplies and have a lot of questions. Just to warn you, those places are like the Secretary of State office. Eat and use the restroom first because you will be there for a while. Or do your homework first and know exactly what you need and what is covered. It will save you a lot of grief in the long run. Trust me.

The next point is this: *touching base on the medical issues, if there is an insurance case management person that your insurance wants to assign to you, let them.* These are knowledgeable nurses with degrees and a lot of experience who can answer all of your health related questions. I was very grateful to speak with this person on my spouse's progress, and she had many helpful suggestions and answered all of my questions. If she could not, she would get the answers.

Here are some other resources I learned about along the journey:

- NYU Medical Center has a lot of interesting educational data for families.
- Virginia has a patient advocate foundation with a compassionate allowance insurance.
- American Health Insurers Plans (works on paying claims quicker for patients).

Regina Hurzlinger is a health care advocate.

Insurance companies can put profits before their patients. If you as the patient do not understand your rights, contact someone who can help or have a family member that can call and get answers for you. Do not assume that because you received a medical bill, you owe it. Billers make mistakes too, and there are many times you should not have been billed or were billed incorrectly. Need someone who can review your health-care bills if you have a high volume of appointments or expensive tests often? Expensive treatment decisions can bring many conflicts of interest. Money spent on patient care is called a loss many times in insurance companies' eyes. Listen carefully… Coverage determination is based on documented medical evidence. It is very important that you have documentation of your visits, *and* you must document the day, time, and person you talk to in all circumstances. If any questions arise later, you have the documentation to fall back on. There is so much to deal with emotionally and healthwise, and when you add in the medical bills that arrive, it's very stressful. And let's not forget the new medications and their costs. These two items I mention—doctor bills and prescription bills—will be a huge additional stressor. Here is the best suggestion I can make: have an advocate and make a binder to categorize the appointments, medical bills, prescriptions bills, costs, and monies paid for all of the above. This organization will make your life easier, especially if you start getting phone calls also. You have the information at your fingertips. If you're tech savvy, you can create spreadsheets also, which is hugely beneficial with all your adjustments.

The next point is this: *try to be nice to each other and patient.* This is difficult as you will argue over stupid things. Remember, they have a lot on their mind and are trying to accept and adjust just like you. Stay strong and pray for strength daily. Remember this: "One day at a time." Trust and communicate your thoughts to each other. Adjust.

The next point is about *family and friends understanding.* As you go through the process, there will be many that may not understand all that you are going through and just how busy and how much time everything takes in your life. You may have to decline an invite if your spouse/loved one does not feel up to it. They may be on medications that make them sick or have bowel issues, or those meds make them extremely tired. Or just being on oxygen can be plain exhausting. People learn to understand this as time goes by as they witness the struggle. It takes a lot of planning to go anywhere with anyone with an illness, especially one on oxygen. They will voice to you how scary it is to worry about not having enough oxygen to drive to an event, stay at the event, and then leave to drive home from the said event. You have to respect this, and as time goes on, you will know with events how long you are able to stay. If someone is sick, has been sick, or has a child that has been sick, you will have to decline going to an event as your loved one has a compromised immune system. And when they get sick, it takes them twice as long as a healthy person to recover.

The next point is about *eating habits*. A person on oxygen cannot enjoy their meals as much as they used to. It takes them twice as long to eat it, then they get frustrated and will eat things that are not has hard to digest. Large numerous-course meals do not come as passionately enjoyed as they used to. As a spouse, you must respect this and have or make meals you want them to enjoy. If they overeat, it is even more uncomfortable for them as they will have a hard time breathing, digesting, and just plain enjoying their meal. Be mindful of this when you are planning meals for both of you. Keep in mind that if you go out to restaurants, you should go off the peak meal times, when crowds are less heavy, and that means less germs. People will stare; that is their nature. This is annoying, but I will say that the more stories that come out in society, the more accepting people are, so to speak, and the less likely they are to stare. Some people will even engage in polite conversation, but most keep their distance. Don't be afraid to still do the things you love. You just have to adjust. Learn ways to still do them!

The next point is about *going out to the movies*. If you enjoy going to the movies, it would be best if you go early on a Sunday morning, when the crowds are not heavy. There is comfortable handicapped seating, and less crowds mean less germs.

The next point is about *vacations*. Inevitable, ours quit to anywhere outside of Michigan because we were waiting for that lifesaving phone call. But like with anything, we adjusted and still found fun ways to enjoy time somewhat away from the constant doctors and all that went with it.

The next point is about your *day-to-day*. For the spouse that keeps working, it is difficult but necessary. You are stressed, but you know you have to go to work. I would very often think of how hard it must be for someone who loved work to not be able to go now. I also think going to work was very important part of my day-to-day.

The next point is about the *things you need to do—for example,* grocery shopping, getting gas, cutting the lawn, raking the leaves, clearing the gutters, cleaning the house/bathroom, doing the laundry, making the bed, making the meals, and snow-blowing. All those are examples of everyday tasks people do, and please don't ever take your spouse or day-to-day life for granted. There were so many things my husband still did in spite of his illness. There is a sense of pride. There will be good and bad days. My husband still did many things even though he could hardly breathe. As a woman, you worry regardless, but you have to let them do some things to a certain extent. They need to still feel important even when they are feeling lousy. Every person's personality is different, every couple is different, and every adjustment is different. You have to respect each other, realize what you can and cannot do, and step up in many situations to make it work. It's compassion and understanding. It's loyalty and trust. It's believing things will get better. I think that like in any situation. There are adjustments; and I hope that I listed enough and placed enough value on respect for each other, communication, and knowing what is best for each of you.

The next point—the final point—is this: it is important throughout the whole adjustment process that each of you make time for yourselves. There has to be alone time for you to try and enjoy the things you enjoy. For the one that is ill, it is possibly a new hobby that requires more sitting and less talking, especially if they're on oxygen. For the spouse, in my case, I made sure to still indulge in time with my girlfriends, including lunch and shopping, yoga, gardening, reading, and just down or quiet time. This is very important to decompress from all the stressors. And another key point is to make sure to do things with other couples and laugh together. This is very important. Never forget you can still enjoy each other's company and "adjust" to everything with laughter and sharing.

Here are some pictures of sharing, laughter, and enjoying life in spite of what it throws at you!

Us enjoying and outside concert with John and Sarah.

Enjoying an afternoon of laugher and beverages with Mark and Amber.

Sharing a lovely summer Day of Historic ships with Angela and Jamey.

At the Tiki Bar for summertime with Roberts Family.

An Unknown Angel's Gift

Robert enjoying summertime at his father-in-laws summer place up North, in spite of the Oxygen.

An Unknown Angel's Gift

Cherie S. Blackwell

An Unknown Angel's Gift

An Unknown Angel's Gift

An Unknown Angel's Gift

Live a life that matters.

Live a life with no regrets.

Make memories.

Spend time with family and friends.

Live, love, and laugh.

Chapter 6

Faith

When you complain, you remain; when you praise, you are raised.
—Joel Olsteen

I COULD NOT LET THIS BOOK be written without mentioning our faith. I believe faith got me and Robert through. Let me give you some background on my religion. I remember my grandmother on my mom's side taking me to church and Bible school as a young girl, and I enjoyed it. I could see how happy all the people were that attended, and it meant a lot to my grandmother. So I knew it must be important. I remember still attending church as much as I could even into my teen years and was baptized at seventeen years of age. I have always prayed and given thanks for all my blessings in life. I found myself praying more and more as Robert and I went on this journey with his illness, always praying for strength most of the time and that he would receive his gift and no longer suffer. Every chance I got back then and to this day, I give thanks for having my prayers answered.

There are so many things in life that you question every day, but I believe that having faith in God making things right will get you through. You have to trust that he is watching and guiding your steps. Robert was raised Catholic, went to a Catholic school, went to church with his family every week while growing up, and also relied on his faith, I believe. However, throughout this journey, I think Robert was losing faith. I think he felt he was being punished for the life he had led for so long. He even said he felt he was being punished. God was making him pay for all his wrongs. I can't speak for Robert and all the thoughts he must have felt throughout this process. I only know that with the support of all who loved him, he made it. I also know that a month before we got that lifesaving call, I said to my husband, "Maybe you should turn to your faith." We did not speak of it again, but I remember that after his surgery, he told me he prayed to God shortly after our talk and said he turned it over to him. He said (in his words), "I cannot do this anymore. I need your help. I am giving up." I cried when he told me this because I am sure that is the reason we finally got that call we needed for his lifesaving transplant and a new lease on life for him and me.

I believe that people should let faith guide them in their daily struggles…and that even when life is going good, you need to thank God for all your blessings. Our prayers were answered, and every morning and night, I thank God for keeping Robert so healthy. I keep the faith that he will continue to stay healthy and never take his gift for granted. We truly are blessed.

When I think of faith, I think of so many definitions, how happy each day makes me, and how faith guides me.

- Faith—it is tried and true.
- Faith—it guides you.
- Faith—believe.
- Faith—trust.
- Faith—do good.
- Faith—be inspired.
- Faith—be loved.
- Faith—love.
- Faith—tranquil.
- Faith—serene.
- Faith—calm.
- Faith—blissful.
- Faith—enjoy.
- Faith—enrich.
- Faith—gush.
- Faith—glow.
- Faith—take time.

- Faith—relax.
- Faith—just be.
- Faith—rest.
- Faith—blessed.
- Faith—it has no end.

All I can say is this: always believe that everything happens for a reason. God has a plan for you, so always keep the faith and ask for guidance. It will get you through each day. Just keep the faith!

Faith is evidence that the best is yet to come.

The next photo is of Robert before and after oxygen… Keep the faith!

The following are some selected pics of Robert's positive attitude from when he was on oxygen leading up to before the lifesaving phone call. We made the best of it!

Took a vacation and made the best of it.

First summer with oxygen on in one of the first family outings. The struggle to breathe is real.

Woodward Dream Cruise.

Making light of the Christmas holiday.
Always keeping me smiling.

An Unknown Angel's Gift

Great-niece Eve's birthday party.

With his brother Mike at an outdoor Gift of Life event.

It's fitting, how this chapter on faith is twelve pages long. This has always been our lucky number ever since one of our first dates when I asked him to play red 12 on the roulette wheel. The first spin, the first gambling hit, the fabulous love of a lifetime... The following BELOW are two shots showing Robert with oxygen before and then after with none. I admired my husband Robert for always staying positive, keeping the faith through thick and thin.

An Unknown Angel's Gift

Family baptism event.
The godfather.

Grateful and Blessed.

Chapter 7

Likes and Dislikes

Keep it simple but unflinching.
—Author unknown

Likes

WELL, HOW DO I TALK about likes during this journey?
First of all, I like that my husband accepted this journey. Was it right away? I don't think so. In fact, I know so. I watched Robert go through so many emotions, knowing full well that on some days, he did indeed have bad days, but he still fought hard not to show me he was having a bad day. Complaining was not part of Robert's vocabulary and never has been. This is a very huge like because when you watch someone you care about feel lousy and not say a word and when they do tell you something is wrong or doesn't feel right, you know it is a reality.

I like that my husband still kept his sense of humor through it all.

I like that my husband still allowed me to schedule social events (and attend them) even though he might have not felt like going anywhere.

I like that my husband still took care of himself even though it was so hard for him to shower, let alone get dressed, with oxygen on and while struggling to have enough breath to complete a task we all take for granted every day. Have you ever watched someone you love or even a stranger struggle with a disease, accept a disease, and live with a disease? It is exhausting. When it is someone you know, you witness their daily moods and the way they handle things. How much patience do they have? How much patience do you have? Do you have someone you can turn to for support? Or do you have faith that will get you through? I have always said to those people out there who complain all the time about simple everyday things, "Go spend time in a lobby at a hospital around sick people [well, wear a mask if you're going to, haha] then stop and think about just how good you have it. If you are living a life, are able to feel well, are in good health, can go to work, can enjoy your hobbies, and can plan fun times with friends and family, well then, you have it pretty good. What if you're struggling with diabetes, cancer, homelessness, joblessness, fighting an addiction, fighting an abusive relationship, or struggling with something? What if you have no one to turn to for help?"

I like that we have many people in our lives that we could turn to for support. I am sure most of you reading this already know this, but I had to reiterate just how important it is to not take things for granted and *like* your life when you have it good and have no real issues to complain about.

I like that I kept my cool, kept my sanity, tried not complain myself, and, on bad days, knew to call on our support system to make me laugh and take me away from the struggle if only but for a moment.

I like that *we* made it through *together*. Robert and I have a strong friendship. When you communicate and trust, you confide in each other and make it. Were there hard times? Of course. Were there disagreements? Of course. Think about all the stress from the appointments, worries, hopes of the future, and thoughts of the future that you will still fulfill your dreams together and that you will battle this disease and win. I look back at present on an entry from December 2008, and wow.

> I pray every day for strength, for Robert, for me. Take it one day at a time.

I like that on December 2009—a year later—Robert opened up to me…and you know it's not always easy for a man to open up.

Yes, he cried. Yes, he needed to. I like the fact that he confided in me. I am sure it was not easy to open up and share. I expressed in my journaling what I said to him: "You can vent to me any time. Cry, scream, talk, whatever you need to do… If it helps, do whatever you need to do to express how hard it must be for that day." I like that people are able to talk one-on-one. I think communication and trust are two of the most important elements in a relationship.

I like the huge support system we had—those who have all been mentioned in an earlier chapter. I thank God for each and every one of them.

I like the very well-educated staff of nurses and doctors that kept us well-informed, the five main doctors being Dr. K, Dr. B, Dr. A, Dr. S, and Dr. N.

I like attending support meetings and gaining not only knowledge from the speakers but also insight from the other pre- and post-transplant attendees. It is amazing what you learn. We especially like the Life Flight (those that would go and pick up the organs for those waiting patients) speakers.

I like that this experience helped me grow as a person and realize just how precious life is. I will never fully understand the thoughts an ill person must have; only they know the struggle. I see it through the eyes of a spouse. I like the fact that I grew a lot in this process. As hard as it was, I know that I learned so much, and I like that.

I like that my husband would still take me out to eat even if he didn't feel like it. I know food and drinks did not taste as well to him. It also took longer for him to digest and was an undertaking that, again, was difficult for Robert.

I like that my husband would still cut the lawn and do his best to take care of household items.

I like that my husband still managed to be extremely kind and giving to others in spite of his condition.

I like the friendship, patience, and kindness he showed me throughout, year after year. I like the honesty and communication that we have always shared.

I like that Robert and I were able to survive such a difficult time through much strength by leaning on each other and others for support.

Thank you, Robert. I like the person you are. Even throughout your illness, you still managed to be an incredible person with an incredible strength that I admire to this day.

I like the way our relationship grew and the extreme amount of respect we have for each other.

I like the way we grew as a couple when enduring what we had to at such a young age, which should not have happened.

Dislikes

I disliked watching Robert struggle when doing numerous walking tests at the hospital to test his breathing/lung capacity. He would push himself event though he knew he was struggling. They would check his vitals, and I would sit there and wonder how he survived the tests when his vitals were so bad. He had tingles in his neck, hands, and feet and felt cold. I prayed he wouldn't not pass out. The staff was always patient, caring, and helpful. I like that! I dislike him getting poked constantly for blood draws. Watching him gave me a new view on so many things. Life is so precious. You have to like all your moments and treasure them.

I disliked knowing how difficult it was for Robert to view me when I would have to do something around the house that he really wanted to do, specifically something a man usually does around the house. Of course, I did not mind doing it, but I know how much he wanted to do it.

I disliked myself for not having the courage to ask him to do something for fear that it would be too taxing on him to do a strenuous activity.

I disliked not cooking as much because it was harder for Robert to get through a meal and enjoy it.

I disliked the ones who looked at us when we were out somewhere together; it was like we had the plague. For the most part, it was something that did not happen very often; and when it did, I held my tongue because I am not one to create a scene. My one granny always said, "Two wrongs don't make a right."

I disliked watching the days, months, holidays, years pass by over and over. Each time I would pull out holiday decorations, or even simple hallmark holiday items, I would wonder will that call come this time.

I disliked getting phone calls from numbers with the 313 area code, only then to realize it was just to schedule a test or give me a result, not that call we had been waiting for.

More about likes

I like that, because of the length of time we waited, more was learned in this field of medicine, and my husband's care was stellar.

And last but not least, I like that I am able to write this book and tell our story of love, the knowledge we gained, the lessons we learned, and the struggle we survived because of so many and our fight to make it work.

The following are more photos to depict the likes and dislikes in our journey.

Thank you.

An Unknown Angel's Gift

Robert with his godchild Zane, four years into waiting for his lungs.

Blackwell Christmas holiday. Five years into the waiting process, Robert always made sure to smile.

Robert and his brother Mike at a holiday gathering, six years into the waiting process.

Robert with his brother-in-law Bill and nephew (by marriage) Scott at my side of the family holiday gathering, seven years into the waiting process.

An Unknown Angel's Gift

Robert enjoying a gift from my family at the holidays at the seven-year mark.

Bill and Joan, Greg and Claudia, Robert and me. One of our dinners many years into the journey, waiting but still enjoying that quality time with family.

I just want to close with one of my favorite likes. As with any journey, time with family and laughter are the best medicines. I am very grateful for this. Time with loved ones and friends is what will get you through a tough time. I like that we can always turn to family no matter what.

Chapter 8

Tools for Growth

Every day, I try to remind myself, to ask myself, "Did I try my best today?"...And I wouldn't be truthful if I said yes...but the will, the spirit, the desire to live, I will never compromise.
—Farrah Fawcett

WHEN I THINK ABOUT GROWTH during this whole process, I think about a support system. You must have a support system in place to get you through.

I have many suggestions for tools for growth, but whether you use them or not is up to you. I can preach to you and say I highly recommend it.

I can honestly say there were many times I did not lean on others when I knew I should have. Many times, I was in tears and scared to death about what our day just held, but I was foolish and did not call a family member or friend; I just held it in and moved on until the next day to see what it held. Maybe I just didn't want to worry the other person and felt my strength would pull me through, which it did. There were other times when I did reach out to family and friends and so glad I did. No matter what kind of questions you may have about the situation you are in with your spouse or loved one, reach out to the doctors, nurses, or any other staff that specialize in that area of expertise if you think you or they need it. Don't be afraid to talk to your loved one if you have concerns. Communication is key. You know your loved one better than anyone, and just reaching out to them and showing concern can help you and them. Obviously, you both know how difficult the situation is—how difficult it is to accept, live with, and learn from. Many people do not understand if they have not been through it. There will be many things you and your spouse can work through together, and a sense of humor will get you through also. Just watching a comedy together or making each other laugh can be a huge help in such a difficult situation.

As a spouse and as a person who found it very difficult to watch my spouse suffer through this illness, I learned that in taking care of them, you must also be sure to make time for yourself. Take time to take care of yourself not just physically but mentally. You must try to rest so you do not get sick yourself. Try to keep the same calendar and continue to get ready each day with drive and motivation. Go to that job, be productive, smile, and greet your coworkers with one. Take time to talk to your friends, make that lunch date, share and let them listen to your thoughts. This is a huge tool for growth because it still shows you can have that time for yourself even while going through a difficult situation. Another tool for growth is alone time, whether it is to sit in quiet, read, take a drive, do yoga, or spend time with younger family members. Kids will always bring a smile to your face even in the hardest of times.

And recommend these things to your loved one who is ill also. Recommend they still see their friends, exercise, and do their best to keep a normal schedule even on days when they feel like they do not want to move. Talk to them and inspire them to want to stay active and not let the disease take control of their lives! Encourage them to stay strong even on days they do not want to, and if you can tell it is a bad day, blow sunshine their way!

Scheduling social events will also help you grow together during this difficult time. Obviously, you will use your judgement and really be considerate as on some days, it really just may be too difficult to attend something. And that is okay. You can't make everything work, but planning a nice afternoon dinner way ahead with family or friends can do a world of good—just sitting and laughing with people who care. This showed us that through all the adversity, we could still have a good time and make the most of the time we had with the oxygen despite the time frame we had to follow. I am very

An Unknown Angel's Gift

grateful to our family and friends for their constant understanding during the years and years of watching what we endured.

I like to think my husband and I are pretty strong people. Throughout the many support group meetings Robert and I attended, we learned that many couples do not make it through and have to separate. You must know that if you have an ill spouse, your life will obviously change no matter what age you are and that when you took your vows, it was for better or worse. Are you strong enough to see it through? This is the person you vowed to love for better or worse. They do not give you an age for this when you take your vows. In our case, my husband became sick six years into our marriage. There was no time following the many years after when we had waited and waited for that call did I think that I should just leave. I think it takes a weak person to leave no matter what age you are. Maybe many people aren't as in love as they think they are and just can't do it. I sympathize. I do. I just know, from my point of view, I was not leaving. I just knew in my heart that we would make it. I believe Robert came into my life and made it better and that we could handle any obstacle.

Be soft. Don't let the world make you hard. Do not let pain make you hate. Do not let any bitterness steal your sweetness. Do not let pain make you hate. Take pride that even if anyone else in the world may disagree, you still believe it to be a beautiful place.

There will be many people (strangers, acquaintances, etc.) you will come across at events who will offer up many opinions. In our case, my husband was waiting for an organ. I will never forget this one instance when an acquaintance said, "We will never be organ donors because I heard that when you come into a hospital, injured, they want your organs. So the doctor will not try his hardest to save your life." Based on the education we have received, we stated that information was incorrect. Doctors have taken an oath to save your life. They do not even know if you are an organ donor when you are brought into a hospital. Thus, this conversation can turn into one topic after another, and it really can turn into an interesting conversation, to say the least. It will be exhausting for both of you. I came to learn over time that it was important for me to explain things as my husband would become winded from trying to explain things. I had no problem doing this. All he had to do was give me a look (communication), and that would be my cue to finish up. Again, there will be many who do not understand at all what you are going through and need a thorough explanation of the path you have had to take, and it helps them understand.

The next items I am about to discuss are huge stressors in the process of having an ill loved one, and you as the spouse should really take care of these or have a family member in place to assist. They're insurance, billing, appointments (including follow-ups), and medications. You have to look at them from a patient's perspective. How would you feel if you were trying to cope with your disease, accept it, understand all there is to know about it, face day-to-day challenges, and then had to deal with insurance companies, questions, and follow-up appointments? To me, being in the medical field, I had no problem with addressing all these issues because I felt my husband shouldn't have to. That is just me. But in my opinion, this is very important in the process. They (the loved one) should not have to worry about bills, talking to insurance companies, trying to understand it, becoming frustrated, and having this worry added to their already worrisome thoughts of trying to stay well (in our case, waiting for a call for a transplant). There will be constant bills coming in. You may not understand them, and if so, you must call and get an explanation.

I think this is one of the most important things as a tool for growth—understanding the process. I created a binder with sections dedicated to doctors' names, numbers, notes, bills, and documented accounts of talks with anyone and follow-up appointments. It will help you considerably in the follow-up. It's a long process, this road you are about to take. And let me tell you this: it's a long one.

That first year can be the most difficult for the patient. They are accepting their disease and trying to move on with life in a different way. You as the spouse (caregiver) of the loved one have much responsibility to keep things afloat. You can do it. I did it. There

An Unknown Angel's Gift

will be calls that frustrate you, but you will get an answer and move on to the next dilemma. You will see a nurse or doctor you may not like. There will be many questions you will think of after. You will eventually get the interpretation you need to understand your many questions whether they are appointment or insurance related. Stay on top of this. There is much money that goes into health-care billing, and many errors will be made. You will save a lot of headaches and problems by staying on top of this. Trust me. This is also very important once your loved one is out of hospital and comes home. It is important, if possible, for the loved one to be on-site when doctors come into the exam room. This is so your questions will be answered. If someone can't be there and the patient isn't alert enough, have them tape the conversation so you can follow up after. This can be a simple recording on a cell phone. My husband did this when I was not there, and we could then discuss together and then call the doctor's office that was consulted for follow-up questions.

You will find just how important it is to have a support system and a main caregiver that can take notes and be there as often as possible. This helps the patient not have to worry so much about every detail. They are trying to heal and are stressed by all the daily demands that get thrown at them for recovery, which involve medications, doctors, nurses, and questions, which happen on a daily basis with hospital stay. Never be afraid to ask questions. This is how you learn and get through each process. You will learn more from asking questions than from going online and trying to understand everything yourself. Pay attention to the patient's concerns, especially if they voice it to you, and ask the staff. Your family member may be on pain medication, sleep medication, and all of the other numerous medications that can make them drowsy. It is a lot to process for them and you.

If you have a religion preference—or even if you don't—and there is a chapel at the hospital, I highly recommend visiting it, praying, and just having some solitude for yourself. You will find it very calming to sit, read the Scripture, and pray. I remember the first time I went to the hospital chapel, and such a calm came over me. The sun came through the window and shined upon my back as I read the Scripture. This is just a suggestion—a very good one, I think.

The next thing I would like to discuss is support meetings. These are crucial to getting through the process. Early on, we met so many pre- and posttransplant patients, and hearing that we were not the only ones going through this was incredible. As with any situation, to be able to talk and share with others who understand what you are going through is a huge de-stressor. It helps you get a grasp on it all somehow if only for a moment. Every single time we went to these, we had gotten something out of it; not only did we meet someone new, but hearing their story was so uplifting and a great learning experience. Here are some examples:

1. An attending gentleman posttransplant with same diagnosis as my husband, Robert, had a transplant and was doing extremely well. He was very helpful. You also see that many of these people have a lot of the same interests; so if but for a moment, you might want to share a happy memory or story of something you both enjoy, which takes the heaviness of your illness off the counter for a moment! Have some laughter, not just tears, to share.
2. I remember a meeting where a pastor came and spoke, and everyone really opened up. There were many tears cried but also some very insightful advice and things I remember to this day. A nurse said she felt very humbled by all of the remarks.
3. I remember the many holiday meetings and the numerous stories of success. To this day, nine years later, there are still attendees we have known since the beginning who continue to attend. It will warm your heart to see people who have succeeded with their illness. Side comment: People succeed when they comply, listen to their doctors, are patient with their caregivers, and are not too hard on themselves. The patient (a family member, spouse, friend, etc.) needs constant support, and you need to be compas-

sionate. Put yourself in their shoes. How would you deal with the situation?

4. I remember a couple vividly who were in the same situation as us, but the female was the patient while he, the spouse, was in same shoes as me. However, he was extremely stressed, and these meetings did him so much good. It taught him coping skills. As a patient, they have to swallow their pride and accept all the numerous changes in their life, and the spouse will get the brunt of their stress. You have to learn to cope and not give up. You have to rely on friends and your own de-stressors, decompress, and have some down time. You as the spouse (family, friend, caregiver, etc.) are their punching bag at times. It's not to an extreme, but there are days where you both have good and bad. You must have communication. Ask them, "What can I do for you to make this particular process we are dealing with right now better? How can I help?" They may say nothing, but over time, you will learn to reach out and know what they may need. Again, put yourself in their shoes. How can you help better this situation?

5. I recall numerous doctors we met in the process who had good bedside manners and lightened the load with kind, encouraging comments, making it not just a doctor-patient visit. And of course, there is my husband with his great sense of humor, who always made the visits so much easier. I am so grateful for that, and I hope you as a caregiver will be that lucky to have someone be as positive and not complain. If they do not complain, it will make your job easier because when they do voice a concern, you will know "Hey, this is real. I need to ask a medical professional what should we do."

6. I recall the many nurse assistants that were so kind and thoughtful, which made the process easier.

7. I could name numerous people we met along the way, especially at meetings, but I think you get the gist of it. We are

grateful to each and every one of them from 2008 to 2015 and until this day as we still go to meetings and still meet pre- and posttransplant patients. It is such a good feeling to know we can help newcomers coming into the process. We always try to give back as all of those people we met over the years were selfless, attending the support meetings and offering advice and guidance as we faced the scariest situation we ever experienced as a couple.

You go through so many stages of moods together, especially during the first and second years. You are scared and concerned, and you're just trying to get through each day! It is indescribable, really. It is difficult. It is an emotional roller coaster. I used this comment many a time at the meetings because you never know what to expect each day, each month, each event, and each phone call, especially after tests have been run. And then you need to make another appointment for another discussion, and there will be another great person you will meet along the way.

At the support meetings we attended, LifeShare and Life Flight coordinators had the best stories to tell, and they were very informative about the part of the process where that call comes in and you get your organ, among others. We are eternally grateful for all the people we met along the way and continue to meet. As a key tool for growth, the people you meet will offer you hope when you think you cannot get through another thing related to the illness. Trust me when I say that you will. And when you do, it will be the best feeling of success, knowing that you made new memories, learned, and grew together throughout the process. My biggest tool for growth? My advice is to never give up. Trust the process!

I suggest packing a bag for the seasons because as you wait for wherever your loved one's illness takes you next, you will have an overnight bag. Place a list on your corkboard or fridge with things to gather when you need to head to hospital (e.g., phone charger, medications, a book, glasses, keys, snacks [crucial]) and make sure your bills are current. Have someone in place who can watch your home.

An Unknown Angel's Gift

A huge tool for growth is planning ahead. Have simple meals you can prepare because you will be busy with appointments, phone calls, and drives to hospital, and you will be tired. Beyond tired, actually. Going through the motions, basically. I remember a friend had made a meal for us while Robert was hospitalized, and I thought that was the nicest gesture anyone could have done.

A very important aspect to all of these tools for growth I have mentioned is discussing with the patient anything that can make their daily life and hospital stays easier—perhaps a crossword puzzle, a good book, music with headphones, or, if they have many sports they like, a TV at their hospital room being in working order. In our case, it was full-blown hockey season. One night, the TV was acting up, and I thought the hospital walls would come down if that was not fixed! I'll talk more about Robert's hospital stay in the upcoming chapters; there was lots of amusement during the stay!

I want to emphasize one of the most important aspects (I feel) for growth: support meetings. Discussions with others who experience the same setbacks, disappointments, and aspirations of the future happen in these meetings. That is the most I can offer as a tool to help you grow. You will be educated on your condition and realize you are not alone in your journey, and it gives you and the patient more to talk about also. I say these parting words in this chapter on growth: Stay tough, stay positive, stay in faith, and call on support; be a survivor!

Games with family—always great for laughter.

Sibling support! Robert with his three brothers pictured here: Jeff, Tim, and Mike.

An Unknown Angel's Gift

Uncle Robert with his nephew Michael and great-nephew (and godchild) Zane.

Bill, Joan, Stephanie, Scott, Robert and me in Kentucky.

Robert and me in our Red Wing attire. Must be watching hockey.

Here's a final thought on tools for growth: Still continue to enjoy the things you love together in spite of what cards you have been dealt! Life is only as good as you make it, so don't sit back and let it slip away. Each day is a gift!

Chapter 9

Our Love Story and the Points/ Situations Leading Up to the Surgery—Life Changing

Something to do, someone to love, something to live for.

Faith is the substance of things hoped for.
—(Hebrews 11:1) Heard via a pastor one day

As I sit here again like I did when I started this book, I thought this book would be just about the lung transplant journey and the illness, then someone suggested, "Why don't you also write about your love story so that everyone can get a glimpse into your life before the illness and not just during the struggle of everything you went through leading up to the moments of the transplant surgery?"

So as I begin this, I anticipate this to showcase a lot of beautiful moments that reflect why we are the strong couple we are, and it's not just because of the illness and the hell it put us through but because of the friendship we built from the beginning with communication and laughter.

When I think back to the day I met Robert, I remember it like it was yesterday, and it was over twenty years ago. He was an acquaintance of my ex-husband, and you know how they say that you'll know when you meet your soul mate? Well, I knew it. He was so mysterious, exciting, funny, and attractive, and he showed interest in me. I knew for a long time that in my current relationship at the time, my now ex and I were on the outs. Robert saved me from more unhappy, useless days. Like I said, I knew full well that the current relationship at that time was done.

Robert and I kept in touch, and talking to him was so easy. He has always been a good listener. I really felt like he understood me, and he knew how to treat me—with respect and kindness. And we soon found we had many common interests. He would write me heartfelt notes, give me cards and flowers, and showed a genuine interest. That was what I needed. I have always found it easy to talk to men and have friendships with men, but with Robert, it was a friendship that was growing. I knew my heart was trying to open up to him, but I was afraid of a relationship. But like I said earlier, I knew he was the one God sent to me. He was someone I could have a real future with. I felt so young with him—and it was such a wonderful feeling to be with someone who genuinely was glad to be with me and around me, someone proud to have a good down-home Southern girl. And my gran, who was a good judge of character, told me early on, "I know that man is going to take good care of you." Robert's mother said I was an angel sent from above.

So as I said earlier in the chapter, there were many phone calls, notes, and long talks. A deep friendship formed with trust and laughter. The many things we enjoy to this day include really nice classic cars; car racing; hockey games; football and baseball games; gambling; war, action, and car movies; a good TV series; a great vacation or adventure; a good drink; good food; spending time with family and friends; laughter; and each other's company. Our first date was at a jazz concert with the people behind us saying, "People, we can't see!" It was quite amusing. I guess there was some smooching going on. The next date included a visit to the casino where we hit on the roulette wheel red 12. I think he fell in love with me then as we kept winning money!

As the months and years continued to fly by, we enjoyed attending many car shows and car races; following Earth, Wind & Fire all over the States; and watching and attending many hockey games together. We have watched many a football and baseball game. We have gambled at places all around the United States, including all in Michigan, Canada, Wisconsin, Connecticut, Maryland, and Las Vegas. We hope to see many, many more in our travels. We have purchased many everyday cars and trucks, and of course, we have our 1966 Platinum Silver GTO *and* 1972 Red Camaro SS. We have watched and been to more movies than we can count. We have seen all of the *007* and *Fast & Furious* franchises at the movies. The many TV series we have enjoyed include *NYPD Blue, Southland, House, Lost, The Sopranos, The Mentalist, Red Shoe Diaries, Deadwood, CSI, Desperate Housewives, Boston Legal, Prison Break, Rookie Blue, Shameless, Californication, Weeds, Breaking Bad, Dexter, Nurse Jackie, The Big C, Ray Donovan, NCIS, Homeland, Survivor, Big Brother, The Amazing Race, Six, Yellowstone, Queen of the South Seal Team,* and *Shades of Blue*.

Let's return back to the early days with Rob. I remember the day I told him I loved him for the first time. I said, "Hey," from across the room. "I do love you." Boy, did he smile big. There are countless memories in the journey that led us to where we are today. I can honestly say that every day, the relationship got better. He always makes me laugh. He keeps me in focus. I remember having a lot of anger and listening to heavier music throughout all my days before I met Robert. Rob gave me a sense of calm and safety, and I even listened to calmer music! However, I enjoy all kinds! We respect each other's alone time. He is my best friend. He respects me, he encourages me, he listens to me, and he completes me.

Robert and I were together for ten years before his illness really grabbed hold of our lives and changed it. In those ten years, we did all the things mentioned above. I enjoy the quiet times together and the simpler things like watching TV, talking, walking hand in hand, going out to dinner, having a good conversation/laughter, Rollerblading, and any outdoor activities. And I love when he grills for us, which he still does to this day.

Each day goes by so fast. You never think when you are a young couple that you will have to deal with an illness, but we were faced with it. Many people do not survive this, but I was in it for the long haul. I knew the strong person Robert was when I met him, and I know the strong person I am because of my life and what I have been through. We strengthened each other. Knowing I am safe and loved is the best feeling there is. I had no doubts when we found out about his illness that he/we would beat it. Because of the friendship we formed, the love we share, and our faith, I just knew we would make it. Sure, there are ups and downs like in any relationship; but when you have built a strong relationship on communication, friendship, and trust, you make it.

When it was suggested that I write about our love story in this book, I thought, *How do I put so many wonderful moments into a book chapter?* When you find someone that you enjoy being with so much, there are not a lot of words to describe it. It just works. We work. I remember when Robert would come home from work and share thoughts with me. I did the same, and I still do to this day. It just works.

As with any relationship, there is euphoria early on, and all I know is I still get excited to come home from the office and see my husband's face even after twenty-plus years. That's pretty good. I have never wavered and never doubted the love we share, the common bond, the common interests, the common goals, and the mutual respect.

I just want to stress how fast time passes—the days, months, and years. You have to cherish every moment. I remember the early years and the different seasons; we were doing all the things we enjoyed, living life, and really cherishing the time together. You just have to look at each other at all different types of moments and know that what you have is pretty great.

It's wintertime. It's cold, the snow is falling, and it gets dark early. You're sitting inside, just watching a TV series, sports, or movies, and you are okay with that. The simple things in life are enough. You eat your meal, and you chitchat. You go out to eat, and you chitchat. You go through the motions of everyday life with the one you love. And it's all enough.

It's spring. The days are longer, and it's lighter out. Now you can go outdoors more, do yard work, go to the park, drive your muscle cars, and take walks. And it's all still enough.

An Unknown Angel's Gift

It's summer. The days are still as long and as light, and you can still enjoy the outdoors together, doing all the things you love including Rollerblading, walking, and cruising, of course. Those are some great times.

It's fall. The days are getting shorter and darker, and you're spending more time indoors again. But that's okay because you are still with the one you love, and even the simplest of times are the best of times.

Many people take every day for granted as well as their love, families, jobs, and health. It's important to look at each day with a grateful heart. I have thanked God every day since the late '90s when he brought Robert into my life. There are not enough words, really, to express how grateful I am for this love that came into my life. Many people never have it; or when they do, they don't appreciate, respect, or know the worth of it. I know the worth of ours, and I will forever spend every day showing Robert how much he means to me.

The first ten-plus years of our relationship were spent enjoying all the things I have mentioned—together creating memories to last a lifetime. Those years were filled with laughter and wonderful times together and with our friends and family.

Other than my grandfathers and father, Robert was the hardest-working man I had ever met. He was early to get to the job and come home. He loved working. You can imagine how crushed he felt when an illness forced him to be unable to go to his job of thirty-plus years any longer. All of the days and memories… The life we made up until this point was put to the test. If you want to test any relationship, throw an illness into it and see how strong that person and their spouse are. If you have the foundation to make it work, it will. You have to be able to communicate and know in your heart of hearts that you will get through.

The next eight years of our love story consisted of many a doctor appointment that you have read about in the chapters leading up to this point. Throughout the eight years of us having to deal with the illness slowing down our living the way we like to live, we learned we are survivors, we are strong, we are fighters, we will beat this and we will "live" again with a new lease, a new outlook. And I can honestly say that the whole process made me look at daily life differently. There is no time for drama or negative people. You still have to live life. I made sure to keep our love alive, and I cannot even believe that to this day, we made it through that wait—that wait for the call that would give Robert a new lease on life. Daily I would just think, *I cannot wait to see my husband enjoying life again without oxygen and with dreams, hopes, and plans for our future… that it will be all right, and that against all odds, you can still be each other's hope to see that light at the end of a long wait. It just has to happen.* I always kept the faith. And you know what? We got that call, that long-awaited call. *Robert is going to feel better,* I thought. *We are about to embark on the surgery and the journey of post-op after the life-saving surgery. We made it through the waiting process. Now let's make it through the hospital stay, the aftercare, and the living of our lives again.*

Here are some pictures of our relationship journey:
Before Robert's illness.

An Unknown Angel's Gift

An Unknown Angel's Gift

2002.

2006.

2008.

2009.

An Unknown Angel's Gift

2010.

2011.

2012.

2013.

An Unknown Angel's Gift

2014.

As we embark on the next chapter of our lives, we must remember that only God knows what the next journey holds for us. And we are ready. And then the call came!

And God surrounded us with strength and determination for the next battle!

An Unknown Angel's Gift

Chapter 10

The Long Awaited Call

When you delight yourself in the Lord, God will give you the desires of your heart.
—Psalm 37:4

LITTLE DID WE KNOW THAT at 9:00 p.m. on December 8, 2015, we would get that long-awaited phone call! God had a plan. An unknown angel was about to save my husband's life. *Warning: This is a long chapter with lots of detail!*

* * * * *

This chapter will amaze you and shock you as I tell of the day-by-day journey of Robert's hospital stay and all the hiccups and bumps along the way. He is a survivor. He is a warrior. He is my husband and someone who I have never admired more for his strength, determination, and sense of humor. Even throughout all he endured, he always stayed positive and tough.

Many times, I will listen to music through my headphones as I write this book; ironically, it is the holidays as I write this chapter. On the night that we got the call and I proceeded to change and get ready for our journey to the hospital, I turned on my holiday music, and "Hark the Herald Angel Sing" came on. I turned on my music again earlier...and this song came on again. It always makes me so emotional because I know just how powerful our God is, and as I sit

An Unknown Angel's Gift

here, hearing it now, I can still remember that night when we got the call and how blessed and thankful we are. He is King.

* * * * *

It was another normal weekday evening at our household; we were relaxing after dinner and watching hockey during the brisk, cold month of December. Robert was doing the dinner dishes, and I was relaxing on the sofa. He said, "Cherie, your phone is ringing," and I just thought it was an update of some sort. However, when I looked down at it, I saw that the number had a 313 area code phone, and our nurse coordinator's name on the screen. I answered and told Robert she was on the phone, and the next words we heard were "We have lungs for you." I think both of us were in shock but were also very hyped up. As you know, we had been preparing and waiting for this call for eight years. We made a couple of calls, and Robert was ready and waiting to drive us to the hospital. I was running around house, checking things on my checklist, and grabbing an overnight bag (one of which I packed for each season of the year). Robert had his coat on and was ready at the door. They wanted us there within an hour. And that was no problem. Robert drove us there (they said the patient should not drive, but I was glad Robert drove).

* * * * *

At *10:17 p.m.*, we arrived. The valet was closed. The parking garage was closed. To the ER parking we went! Dad and Claudia beat us there; they were waiting with a wheelchair and warm greetings! We were taken to the ICU—*room P541*. Devin was the nurse prepping Robert and giving him his IV. Gwen, another ICU nurse, came into the room to talk with us. At *11:00 p.m.*, we are waiting for Dr. N (Robert's surgeon) to come in to speak to Robert and have him sign two consent forms. At *11:38 p.m.*, Visna (one of the best nurses we have ever met and will never forget; she was Dr. N's third hand) took a video of me cutting Robert's ponytail. This was what he wanted: to have me cut his hair on the day of his surgery and donate it. It was a touching moment—us in that hospital room, looking at my husband in that bed, wondering what was going through his head as he lay there, waiting for a life-changing surgery. In that moment, there was still great conversation and laughter among us and the nurses. I can remember it like it was yesterday. Before departing to the operating room, Robert's blood pressure was 168/95—the highest I had ever seen it. No anxiety medications were given. Robert was handling things quite well. At this point, Dr. N came in to go over a few key items with us and had Robert sign the two consent forms.

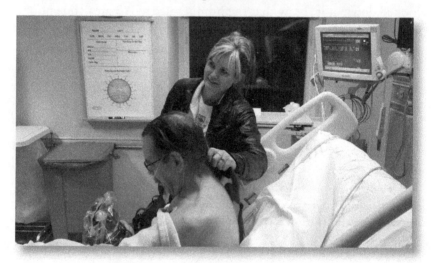

Here is me cutting Robert's hair.

What a touching moment this was. Thank you to the nurse that filmed it.

And then...okay, Cherie, do this.

An Unknown Angel's Gift

As we walked down what seemed like the longest hallway I had ever been down with Robert in a bed and all the nurses close to it, I realized it was time. Time to see my husband being taken through the big double doors and rolled down into surgery. I told him, "You're not allowed to look at any light. You are to stay here with me. We have a lot of living to do, and I love you." Everyone wished Rob well, and off the rest of us went for what would be a very long night. I always said that when this time came, I would stay awake the whole time, and that I did. I held on to Mom and Dad Blackwell's rosaries.

At *11:45 p.m.*, I was informed that the donor was being pulled from life support. I felt an enormous amount of sadness for that family's loss at that moment, and I also had a grateful heart to know someone out there (an unknown angel) was saving many lives tonight and giving many a precious gift.

At *1:10 a.m.* on December 9, 2015, Rana, one of the many nurses I met, said that the lungs were on their way and that the doctor had made his incision.

At *1:47 a.m.* on December 9, 2015, Rana informed me that the lungs had arrived and that the doctor was still working on Robert. I remember telling the family, and I remember feeling as if I had so much love and faith around me. I truly believe that every guardian angel was at my side at that moment, saying it was going to be all right. I held Mom and Dad Blackwell's rosaries and continued talking to Dad and Claudia as well as Mike and Lori (Robert's brother and sister-in-law). We were all there for one another that night. I never slept. I would not sleep. I just kept praying continuously. Claudia and I took Robert's clothes to the truck. It was a quick walk. I thought, *This does not seem real.* It was like a dream. But it was real. We all sat there together. All I could think of was Robert lying on that table with that clamshell incision and all the doctors and guardian angels in the room with him, knowing he was going to come through this like a champion—all smiles and full of strength.

At *2:47 a.m.* on December 9, 2015, all was okay, as per the nurse.

At *3:00 a.m.*, I had a side note to my husband, Robert: I just thought of that Eminem song "3 a.m." It made me chuckle because I thought of the way you and I poke fun and sing that song!

At *3:10 a.m.*, I took pictures of us exhausted ones. We are all slap happy at this point.

Dad, me, and Claudia at *3:14 a.m.* on *December 9, 2015*.

Lori (sister-in-law) and me at *3:15 a.m.*

Lori was helpful in suggesting I keep people updated, and she was right. To every text or phone call that came in, I was replying, and the phone was constantly blowing up. There was lots of love, prayer, and wonderful support.

Journaling…it was exhausting.

An Unknown Angel's Gift

My Nike shoes looked pretty cool—"Just do it."

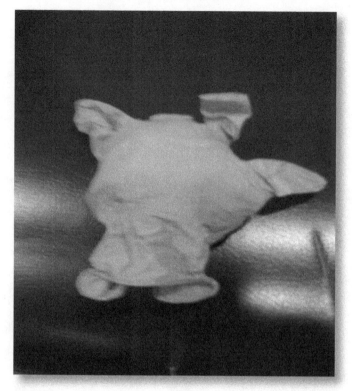

Take another picture. As you can see, my socks
are off. See the next notation.

I was so tired, and for some reason, I walked into the restroom without shoes. Lori said, "You can't keep those and put them back on. Take them off. They are contaminated." I said, "Yes, these bathroom floors and other floors are dirty." So we put my dirty socks in some exam gloves, and then we tossed them. It was a pretty funny moment.

An Unknown Angel's Gift

Brother Mike slept through some of the shenanigans. *However...*

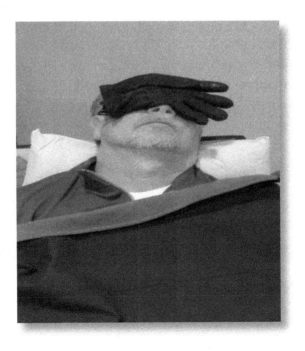

At this point, at *4:28 a.m.*, Michael said in his sleep, "It's surgery. You need bigger gloves!" And at *4:31 a.m.*, he said again, "You need bigger gloves!" Maybe he meant he needed bigger gloves to cover his eyes from the bright hospital lights.

At *4:36 a.m.* on December 9, 2015, we got a call from Nurse Rana. Everything was going very well.

At 5:00 a.m., I was still awake, praying and thinking of Robert and all the love I have in my heart for him!

Two hours passed, and there was no call. It seemed like forever.

At *6:51 a.m.* on December 9, 2015, we got a call from the nurse. The doctor was closing. He would come see us when able.

The sun was coming up. I remember this moment like it was yesterday. In my heart of hearts, I knew everything went very well and that my strong, courageous husband was doing very well. I felt such a strong sense of the presence of angels around us all. I just knew in this moment that all was good and that all was going to be fine, and I also knew just how blessed we were! Thank you, heavenly Father, for guiding that surgeon and all his assistants as they placed an unknown angel's lungs inside my husband and gave him a new lease on life. I could not wait to see him and tell him I loved him and how proud I was of him.

At *7:00 a.m.*, my brother got here, and I was so glad he came by. He lifted my spirits and gave me extra support.

Me and my brother Bill. So grateful for my brother Bill's support.

An Unknown Angel's Gift

At *8:00 a.m.*, Dr. N, the surgeon, came and spoke to me, and he told me how well Robert did. He did say that the early portion of the surgery was the most crucial as Robert's lungs had shifted over in front of the heart and adhered to the chest wall. He had to put him on the heart-lung bypass machine so he could "scrape" the old diseased lungs off his chest wall, which took over an hour, close to two. Once he got the old diseased lungs out, he said everything went very well. He would be put into the ICU room, and we would be able to see him. Dr. N texted me some pics of the old lungs.

Day 1 after the surgery
December 9, 2015

At *10:30 a.m.*, Robert was placed in an ICU room: P558.

Mike, Lori, and I were with Robert until after noon. Side note: I prepared myself to see someone looking pretty rough with all the Prednisone, but *he* looked great in spite of what he had been through. There were more IV poles then you could imagine, monitors, and nurses, and there was constant monitoring. I knew the nurses' names already and the shift plan from looking at their boards.

Robert's friend Jamey arrived at *12:30 p.m.* and stayed until 5:00 p.m. Robert's brother Tim arrived and stayed during this time frame.

Cousin Guy came by at *2:00 p.m.* What a pleasant surprise. Robert was doing very well to be day one and happy to have visitors; just tired, but looking very well. (Robert, *from 1:00 p.m. to 3:00 p.m., they turned your vent off. You were breathing on your own, but you still looked a little concerned. No need, I knew in my heart of hearts that you were going to be fine.*) There were so many guardian angels around. I felt a strong sense of comfort.

Here is a picture of Robert after coming out of surgery (it's hard to explain what this feels like seeing a loved one hooked up to so much!):

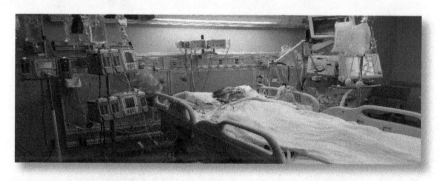

An Unknown Angel's Gift

In the meantime, all of Robert's vitals, x-rays, blood draws, blood gas analyses, etc. looked *great*—no surprise. And his coloring was even better...finally!

At *5:00 p.m.*, Robert's vent was pulled. Robert was adamant about it being pulled, but he was awake and ready. Here I was, the nervous one, but he was looking to his friend Jamey for support, saying, "Get it out!" Well, out it came, and he was breathing well! And then he asked me if his lungs were normal. He was still a little out of it, I think. I said yes. Robert kept telling me how sore his arms were and asked me to please rub his arms.

It had been thirty-two hours since our arrival at the hospital...and I was still up. Jamey offered to drive me home, and I accepted. As much as I did not want to leave Robert's side, I knew I needed to go home, even if briefly. I placed a hand kiss on Robert's forehead and went home.

At *6:30 p.m.*, I was home, and I hated that Robert, my love, was not here. Looking around, I knew I should rest, but my mind was racing a mile a minute. So here was what I did. I tidied up some and ate a bite.

At *7:30 p.m.* was the nurses' shift change! And this was when I was informed by my wonderful sister-in-law (Lori) to call to get updates (during their shift changes!). Everyone had been a huge support in assisting me, socializing, and making sure I ate! Robert was doing well. At *8:30 p.m.*, I spoke to Kylie, Rob's nurse, and she said Robert was doing very well. They would take out the PICC and groin lines in the morning!

I wrote a late-night note to Robert... He was there, and I was here.

> I hate being away from you, but if I am there,
> I would dote on you. And you need your rest!
> Good thing I came home—delivered package
> and cats are hungry!

You cannot even imagine the sense of joy and pride I felt today and the love I felt for Robert and his strength. In case anyone who knows us did not already know, he is my knight in shining armor, and I just love him.

It was a very emotional day, watching Robert breathe so well. For hours, I watched him breathe so freely and so gently; there was no struggle. This was a gift he *deserved*. Robert's mother always said he was special, unique. Anyone who knew him knew this. He truly was an amazing, strong human being. God had blessed him. God had blessed us.

We had a lot of living to do. I could not wait to see Robert shift the muscle car. That would make my heart melt. Like the easy breaths I saw Robert take today, shifting that car and living life each day to the fullest would come just as easily.

Day 2
December 10, 2015

In the early morning on the tenth, I was up, and I had called the hospital at 6:00 and 6:45 a.m. Robert was doing well, and some lines were still there as anticipated. I would venture down to be with him. Thank goodness for my friend Pat R, who was watching over the house and taking care of the cats.

At *9:00 a.m.*, I was at the hospital. The drive downtown was not bad as the weather was mild for December. I was so blessed and lucky for this! Robert was sitting up. *What!* He was doing very well and orientated.

Working those lungs!

An Unknown Angel's Gift

At *10:00 a.m.*, he was sitting up and sipping liquids too, but none of the adult beverage variety!

At 11:00 a.m., *no oxygen*!

I spoke to Robert's brother Jeff today and his niece Kristyn with updates.

Robert had asked me to rub his arms as they were so sore. We both got *some* rest in the morning.

At *11:00 a.m.*, someone from the insurance case management, Jocelyn, came by to gather information and talk with us extensively. It was mentioned that we would go home with a nebulizer and a discussion of home health care. It was pretty exhausting work to converse! By 11:30 a.m., I had a migraine. But I took a pill, and it vanished by noon!

I was looking rough on day 2! Not a glamour shot!

As we move on, only on day two did Robert ask to see his lung pictures. "*Wow.*"

At *12:25 p.m.*, I asked Robert, "Have you taken a *deep breath*?" Robert said, "It's not like they say it is. It's the hardest thing I have ever done." Rob said that when he went to try to rest, it was like he'd forget to breathe! It seemed hard to take a deep breath or breathe normally, but he was trying. He stated that his abdomen felt painful.

At *12:30 p.m.*, Robert's brother Mike arrived, and it really cheered Rob up. He and Mike had a great connection, and I was so glad he had him to talk to!

At *2:30 p.m.*, Robert's brother Jeff arrived, and it cheered Rob up even more. Jeff was another great connection and great conversationalist.

At *4:00 p.m.*, my dad arrived! Here was another person to lift Robert and my spirits! There was so much to absorb while in the hospital. Everyone that came by was signing Robert's heart and lung pillows.

At 5:00 p.m., the nurses told us that Robert was off the insulin. Okay, let's see about that!

At *6:30 p.m.*, one of Robert's first nurse coordinators came to visit—Lauri.

Between 7:00 p.m. and 8:00 p.m., Robert's great friend Jamey and his daughter Ashley came to visit. They were such great people!

After the visitors left, Robert and I watched hockey and relaxed. Robert told me he was seeing spots and having hallucinations. We told the nurse. They stopped the morphine and went to oral pain meds (oxycodone, Tylenol, and Xanax). It seemed to improve over time. In the meantime, also, the nurse practitioner removed Robert's IV from his right forearm as he said it was very sore.

At *1:00 a.m.*, Robert told me how sore he was and said that he might have overdid it, and he said he was going to try to rest now. I said, "Okay, honey, let's rest now!"

At *1:40 a.m.*, I woke up (there were background noises in the hall). I remember just looking over at Robert (they had a nice sofa in the ICU room for family!) and watching his chest expand with every breath! This was truly amazing! He was resting comfortably! I was sitting in dark, trying to be quiet. I remember journaling this as I type it now for the book.

God bless him for this truly *amazing gift!* Today was the day the Lord had made. Today was a new day. *You got this, Robert,* I thought.

Day 3
December 11, 2015

Wakey-wakey...

At *5:30 a.m.*, we had a beautiful nurse named Chelsea come in. Rob woke up briefly (to check her out—haha, just kidding), and his heart rate and blood pressure were up...because of the stress of it all, as per the doctors. They gave him Lopressor, and by 6:00 a.m., he was resting again.

At *7:00 a.m.*, Robert was up and sitting up in a chair! (*Side note: This is a very stressful time for me: when they get him out of bed before he has enough strength. There are tubes everywhere, and it takes much maneuvering to get him comfortable!*) He has had his breakfast and cleaned up.

At *8:00 a.m.*, Dr. N (Robert's surgeon) and a colleague came to visit Robert. They stated to have the chest tube removed within an hour—around 9-ish.

At *9:00 a.m.*, Dr. A (chief pulmonologist) and a *physical therapist stopped by.* The neck tube was not out yet.

Here are some pics I took for day 3 before I popped on home for a bit...

After this, I ventured out...

Oh, the snack and gift shop at the first floor before elevators? It's a life saver. Don't mind if I do—a banana. I left and picked up more headache medication! I took at two-hour nap! I showered and made it back before dark (5:30 p.m.) (the daily plan), got back to the parking spots by the entrance, and was in the door and up to room before dark!

The visitors today (day 2) were the following: *11:30 a.m.*, Bill; *12:30 p.m.*, Mike; *1:00 p.m.*, Patty (one of first nurse coordinators); and *6:30–8:30 p.m.*, Dad and Claudia.

I got rid of my headache early! Robert produced sputum today, which made the doctors happy!

We took our first selfie and had our first kiss!

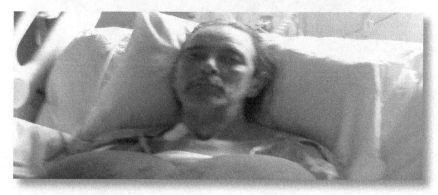

Sleep well, love. The tube is out of your neck!

An Unknown Angel's Gift

Day 4
December 12, 2015

Well, Robert and I both slept well through the night. We were up early with a beautiful nurse on shift today (Heather from Fenton!). Robert washed his face and worked on his blows. We brushed his hair, and I put it up for him! We were waiting for the physical therapy team to arrive. It was early!

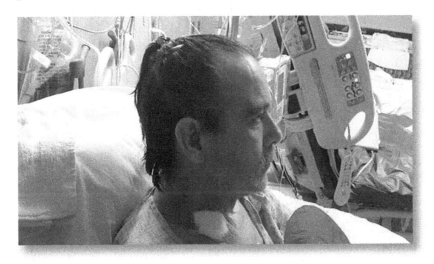

Well, it turned into a rough morning.

At *7:30 a.m.*, as they tried to get Robert up and into the chair, his legs were very wobbly, and no success. *And* half of his chest tube (he had two on each side) came out at the middle of the connection, but it did not come loose from his chest—thank goodness. But the nurse screamed when it came out of the connection. I just about had a heart attack. At this point, they had things back in place, and Robert sitting up in bed for an hour and was quite aggravated. His heart was jumping around, and he had low blood pressure. They gave him extra fluids and Lopressor, and he started looking better and more calm. This was very stressful. I texted family members quite a bit this morning, and they helped so much. Robert was very tough, as everyone knew, and had jumped hurdles in three days. He was being hard on himself. In my opinion, that oxycodone was nasty stuff. It made patients very groggy. No hallucinations, though, like with morphine, but Robert was more coherent on the morphine, if that makes sense.

At *9:20 a.m.*, all of Robert's numbers appeared normal again, and at *9:50 a.m.*, Dr. N said he would like to prescribe Amiodarone for the irregular heartbeat that was happening. Rob was just so exhausted. I hated stepping out, but I knew I should to just go decompress and maybe eat something.

At *11:00 a.m. to 12:30 p.m.*, I made some calls, placed some texts, then took a break. After coming back upstairs, I learned Robert ate a good lunch of roast beef.

At *1:50 p.m.*, Robert's chest tube number 2 was out. Yay! My hero. And we napped from *2:00 p.m. to 3:00 p.m.*!

At *6:00 p.m.*, Robert was resting comfortably. As you can see, he really enjoyed the applesauce. It works great to put your pills in that; it's so you don't have a crappy medication taste in your mouth!

At *4:00 p.m. to 5:20 p.m.*, Mike and Lori brought us Mr. Chicken! Rob was sitting up in a chair, eating dinner.

What a busy day! (Side note: Just run some hot water, put it in a bowl, and put the person's hand in it; and they will use the urinal... Well, wasn't that just too much information! But it works. Tell your friends and family! Success! *)*

Mike visited at *7:00 p.m. to 8:00 p.m.*, and again, as always, he helped Rob so much!

At *9:00 p.m.*, Robert was back in bed again. It had been a very long exhausting day.

Rob told me something very heartwarming today. It would make you think. He said he told God last week he was tired and that he was ready. He was giving it to God. This made me so happy to hear this that I cried, as I recently asked him last month to turn and look to his faith in God.

By *9:30 p.m.*, Robert and I were eating ice cream and having great conversations.

Day 5
December 13, 2018

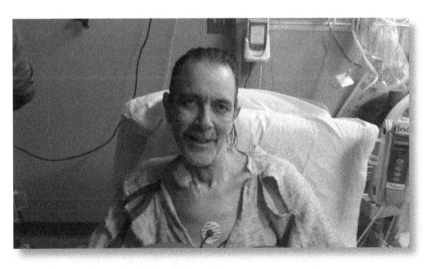

"Don't I look great!"

Robert was sitting up, out of the bed, in a chair! His hair was washed, and he had some breakfast. But I was still exhausted! He told me, his wife, so!

Robert even had a few visitors again today:

- Jamey and Angela (great friends)

- Bill and Joan (brother and sister-in-law)
- Jeff (Robert's oldest brother)

He was started on Prograf.

I went and stayed home from 11:30 to 4:30 p.m. today.

I was then back at the hospital. For those three to five hours a day, I'd go home to tidy up, pick up groceries, open mail, write bills, make us food... Well, there was not time for rest. I just rolled with it and went through the motions, but I was tough. Just seeing how tough Robert was would make my day every day.

I heard Robert did really well today! This was an exceptionally memorable evening, as Robert and I just sat for four hours with no television and just talked. It was real quality time together. You really learn how much you love a person when you just go through something, and you sit and spend quality time without media or television to entertain you.

Thank you, God, for this person in my life. Thank you, God, for the gift of life.

Day 6
December 14, 2015
Room P522

By *5:00 a.m.*, both of us were awake! Rob said he awakes at 3:00 a.m.!

At *6:00 a.m.*, Robert was sitting up in bed, eating a big breakfast with eggs, toast, and coffee. Robert had a good attitude today. He took his medications well. I was very impressed with him. (*Side note: no stomachache today!*)

At *9:00 a.m.*, Dr. A came by to consult. Fides and Christine (the nurse coordinators) came to visit and brought a lung pillow for Robert to hug against his sore chest, and visitors could sign it. Robert's Prograf medication dosage was decreased today.

Robert's favorite word through all of this was *wow*. His quote was "Another day of 'I don't know' and 'Wow'!" We still laugh about this because every day was "a day of wow"—from things said by staff members to actions to the things Robert and I said to each other and the staff! We kept it real and amusing! He said that during the last two days, he wanted to say *fuck*, not *wow*, because he was so lightheaded when went to get up. The oxycodone made him lightheaded, he thought, because he took it before meals, and then he had the dreaded bowel issues.

At *9:40 a.m.*, I noticed that Rob's heparin midline came out of his left arm. He had blood all over arm. The nurse retaped it. I mentioned how it looked, but they said it was a good thing I noticed it came out so they could come in and replace it.

At *10:30 a.m.*, Robert had breathing treatments. Breathing treatments were fun! I had to mask up if I stayed in the room while Robert did these!

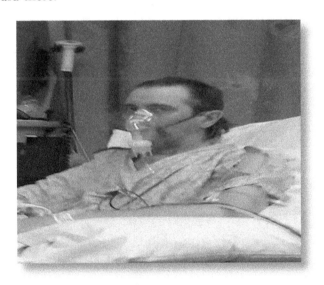

At *11:00 a.m.*, Robert's great friend Jamey called for an update.

At *11:45 a.m.*, Robert's nurse today, May, replaced his arm line for an IV needle. What a great nurse. He needed a new one!

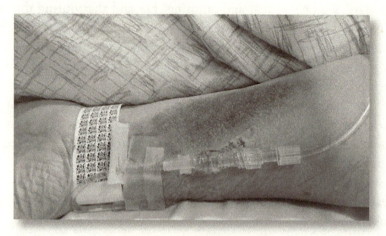

Daily pain endured by my hero

Pour yourself a drink, put on some lipstick, and pull yourself together.

Liz Taylor

An Unknown Angel's Gift

The new nurse was in today—Mia. We had not seen her yet today. It was a really busy day in the ICU.

From *1:00 p.m. to 2:00 p.m.*, Mike, Dad, and Claudia came by.

At *3:00 p.m.*, Nazir, the physical therapist, came by to get Robert out and about.

I was a bundle of emotions during this whole process; however, I did not show it to Robert.

I would wait until I went downstairs to decompress or drive home to feel my emotions take over—more like tears of joy because I was so proud of him.

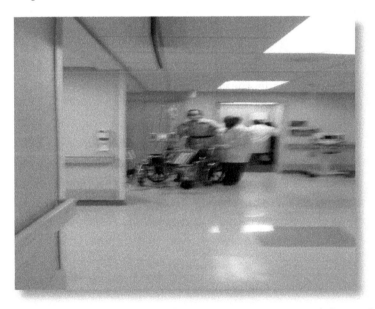

Robert did great; however, his emotions were up and down also. Surely, this was because of the Prednisone and all the stuff they were throwing at him! They were pushing him do the foot pedal at bed also. After his walk, he was back in bed and fell asleep within five minutes. He said he was exhausted! One thing's for sure: when you are in the hospital—whether you're a patient, a visitor, or a caregiver—you have to grab the *zs* when you can as you'll never know when someone will walk in, wanting to check something or administer it!

His first outburst to me today made me realize that the hospital food was not cutting it! His words were "Get this shit outta here," and he pointed to the food tray on his table, motioning to me! Oh boy, this was gonna be fun.

At *5:00 p.m.*, I went for a walk to the hospital lobby, the gift shop, and the cafeteria. I was gone for an hour. I think Robert truly missed my company. He said he was telling the nurse how we met twenty years ago, how I saved him, and how I was his angel.

At *7:30 p.m., we were quite cozy, watching the hockey game!*

At *9:00 p.m.*, they decided to move us to another room. Really, they had to move us now? They said they needed the ICU room he was in at present. I thought they moved him too soon, but that was just my opinion. And everyone has one.

Here was our step-down unit: room 522. This was a nightmare. I remember us moving, the volunteer ramming the bed into the doorway twice, and Robert saying, "Wow." And we were laughing even in the midst of it all. This room had no monitor screen. They said, "You get a pocket form." There was a bathroom, but we still asked for a bedpan as it wasn't easy to ambulate based on Robert's location!

Robert was quite amusing that night. He told me after we were in the room to call this chapter "Kiss My Ass and Call It a Love Story"! This experience was mind-blowing. I had the giggles that night.

An Unknown Angel's Gift

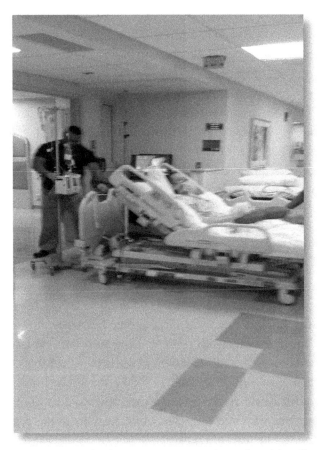

At *10:00 p.m.*, I had an anxiety attack. I should call a doctor maybe. Okay, not... I just had to breathe.

I literally had to hit the restart button on the drip pole as they were beeping constantly and Robert wanted me too. He had a bend in the line. It was time for a shift change, so we didn't count on anyone checking it too quickly. They were getting updates before they started with next round of patients. We had a nurse named Elinor. Rob said he was not sure if he wanted to even get up; he said, "Not trusting these yo-yos today in this section of the hospital."

Day 7
December 15, 2015

Bright and early in the morning, we were told no water was allowed this morning as Robert's sodium level was low. He was offered apple, grape, or grapefruit juice. Rob said, "I cannot have grapefruit juice." We looked at each other.

Breakfast came, but it is all wrong as we were in a different area. And they had no idea. Robert got a new tray of food, and there were mighty shakes. This made Robert happy. Laura was our new nurse.

At *10:00 a.m.*, Jocelyn, the case manager, came by with a nebulizer and filters to discuss about when Robert would go home. The blue book was introduced today. The new nurse, Samuel, was on and mentioned about giving insulin as needed. Robert's white blood cell count was 16 yesterday and was now 18.8 today. He had no fever. His blood pressure was 108/66, his heart rate was ninety-three beats per minute, and his oxygen reading was ninety-six percent. They must have expressed a lot of concern today, and this must be why I logged these numbers.

I left to go home from *1:00 to 5:00 p.m.* today. I talked to Terri M. today, our nurse at our primary care doctor office. I always tried to call someone different each day while away from the room to give people updates instead of texting.

I went back, and it looked like an evening of peace and tranquility.

We were called the comedy couple!

Get your coffee and paper and get up! The commode has arrived!

An Unknown Angel's Gift

Day 8
December 16, 2015

It was *5:00 a.m. Yeah, wakey-wakey, you two! The sun is up, and your nurses are ready to roll, Robert! Lights on. Thank God for my eye mask... Everyone knows what a morning person I am.* Days passed so quickly, though, and I quickly woke up bright-eyed and bushy-tailed to see what they had in store for my husband today! There were so many processes, and they had a plan I was sure they followed for all patients. But not all patients are the same. This is so true with patients and their recovery journeys. If you're a prelisted patient, a postlisted patient, or even a support member, you know how difficult the journey is and that *every* person heals differently and at a different pace. I can say that at this moment, be patient, strong, and confident. Most of all, be positive and supportive to the patient going through it. There are many emotions, changes, and adjustments to not only the body but also the mind and spirit.

When I think of many different health situations, I try to put myself in that person's shoes (switch the spots, so to speak). How well would I deal with this as the patient? I can tell you that a person really learns their strengths and weaknesses. I can tell you that what the patient needs is for their support person to really listen to them, communicate, and respect their needs. They also need patience and understanding. When you watch your loved one struggle, recover, and fight, it really shows you their strengths. The support person will learn what they need at this time also. Pay attention to your health during the patient's recovery. If I am repetitive in this, well, forgive me, but it is just as important for you reading this as a support person to know when to stop, evaluate the situation, decompress, and think about what the best thing for you to do or say in that moment is. If you're ever not sure, visit the church chapel. You will get any answers you are looking for there. He is the light and the way.

Now Robert's vitals were okay today for 5 a.m.: blood pressure of 117/63, oxygen level at ninety-four percent, and a pretty low pulse and heart rate—sixty-four beats per minute. The medicine slowed things down a bit. He was at 180 pounds. Just as Robert is trying to relax and rest… at *7:30 a.m.*, two gentleman came to transport Robert to the fourth floor for a bronchoscopy. One of these gentlemen did three tours in Iraq and one in Afghanistan. We thanked him for his service. During the whole time in the hospital, it was so cool to meet all the different types of people in the staff. Most were personable and happy, and what a difference that made to wake up to people who cared in a hospital setting. It's really cool if you just stop and listen to what people have to say. They can be really interesting. They're not just a beautiful face but someone who leads an interesting life. How many of us can say we meet people every day who challenge us, inspire us, and make us want to be better? We did—Robert and I—every day: from assistants to cleaners to nurses to secretaries to doctors.

*While Robert was gone, I freshened up, sat back, reflected, and looked outside (*I always took time every day to look out the window and thank God for watching over us and directing Robert's healing steps*). And now I sat quietly* if but for a moment, listening to Earth, Wind & Fire (one of our favorite bands), waiting for Robert to return.

Every day at sunrise from the Hospital Room.

An Unknown Angel's Gift

At *9:30 a.m.*, Robert was back, and he was exhausted, understandably. His blood pressure was 111/62. He was resting comfortably. He was fading in and out and telling me (while he was resting) how he was praying the whole time. This made me smile. I drew a picture of a hand, thumbs up, next to this revelation he mentioned. He said the surgeon and head pulmonologist came by and said his bronchoscopy looked good!

At *11:30 a.m.*, Robert's blood pressure read 99/58. Yes, that's Robert's, not mine (I was the one with those kinds of readings usually). His O_2 was at 96 percent and his heart rate was ninety-two beats per minute. Fabulous.

At *noon*, Robert's blood pressure was 101/54.

Dad and I left to go to the lung transplant holiday gathering. What an amazing turnout as always for December. Gift of Life and a News Crew were in attendance as well as numerous pre- and post-transplant patients. Everyone shared their stories, including me. I broke down and said, "After eight long years, Robert finally got his transplant." You should have heard all the *aww*s and gasps in the room. Dad and I were very emotional. He stood up with me and placed his arm around me. He had been the best support system. We could never thank him enough.

As we walked back to Robert's room, I reflected on so much. How could you not? When you hear so many inspiring and uplifting stories of the ones who have been to hell and back and lived to talk about it and think of all the things they are doing that they never thought possible again, you realize it is a true gift—a blessing. There are so many unknown angels out there that put that heart on their license and made the choice to donate their organs. To them I say, "Thank you."

While Dad and I were gone and at the meeting, an occupational therapist came and got Robert up, and he walked to the restroom!

They were not letting him drink very much because of a low sodium issue, and he was not happy! He just told the nurse, "I am in the dessert"! He was being very demanding and bossy (haha, and I don't blame him)! We laughed about it, of course, and I called him the general. I let him rest, and Dad headed home.

An Unknown Angel's Gift

I ventured down to the cafeteria, which was so strange, by myself, but I was okay. I felt like this experience made me a much stronger, more confident person. I made a call to a friend, Pat D, and saw a field mouse run across the floor!

Yuck! It was amusing and gross at the same time.

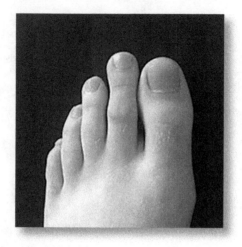

All I could think of while sitting there, talking, trying to eat, was the mouse running across my feet, hahaha. Everyone I talk to said, "Welcome to the hospital cafeteria," after this story told!

I was back at the room and happy to see my husband alert. He'd miss me when I stepped away!

Day 9
December 17, 2015

It was *5:00 a.m.*, and Robert's nurse today was Chen-Yu! Wake up! Robert said he felt really good today, and he sounded good. He had a new IV line placed today, and he was very happy about that!

It was *6:30 a.m. Good morning!* His blood pressure was 116/67. His oxygen was 96 percent. His heart rate was seventy-four beats per minute. (Man, even as I write this today, these early-morning wake-up hours were brutal on both of us!) The nurse's assistant came in, and he was like a marine. He said, "I am here on blanket patrol, Sargent Blackwell!" Robert was out of it and said, "What are you doing here? What do you want?" He was then coherent and given slight assistance to make it to the restroom today.

Shortly, later in the morning, Robert was taken for an x-ray. I left to go exchange the slippers I bought Robert and go home. It was forty degrees out in the D. What a mild December in Detroit, Michigan!

At *5:00 p.m.*, I was back right on the dot before dark, and the "creepies" came out. Robert and I had a nice dinner. He just loved my cooking, and we had a really nice talk too. They had put his "suction" back on as his x-ray showed some collapse on one side. Today, the nurse showed me how to pound on Rob's back. He really liked this. It helped him feel much better. This became a daily ritual (treat) that I did for my husband.

At *7:30 p.m.*, Robert's evening nurse was Denise, and we did not like her. She was late with everything and not as personable as the others. This was the one and only time his medications were late (by one and a half hours)! We continually asked where they were. We could hear all of the nurses' pagers going off all night. They had a very busy night. They had such long shifts. I do not know how they do it! This was Rob's quote of the day today: "And now for something completely different!"

Day 10
December 18, 2015

At *5:45 a.m.*, Robert and I woke up early. We had success with ordering breakfast by 6:30 a.m.; however, we were still waiting for it at 7:55 a.m. He was very hungry. Well, we had success again with the commode, so that was a plus for anyone day to day, let alone someone in the hospital. Rock star strength. I do not even remember if breakfast actually showed this day. However, I did go down to get us breakfast—cold cereals—which worked fabulously. We enjoyed our "fun" breakfast cereals together!

Dr. H (fellow) stopped in to tell us his x-rays still showed some amounts of fluid and that the air was coming out, so they scheduled a bronchoscopy in one month for surveillance only and did a biopsy to make sure there were no signs of rejection.

By *11:00 a.m.*, the occupational therapist arrived to help Robert with endurance and mobility. Robert was very crabby today. Robert was talking to both of us, and he and I were asking questions. He then proceeded to scream at me, "I am not talking to you!" I, as his wife, just love the Prednisone effect. The therapist proceeded to tell him, "Conserve your energy and take your time, Robert." She then proceeded to say, "I am going to leave you in a fully capable nurse's hands," and looked at me like I was imposing on her visit. *Really? I am the spouse, lady, and have concerns like anyone else.*

This was a very hard day for me. The therapist, Michelle, was quite rude to me. I thought, *Whatever.* We had to know the process, so asking questions was normal. Maybe I was just unusually sensitive, or maybe I wasn't. But at any rate, that was no excuse to be rude to the caregiver. She probably thought, *Well, her husband is yelling at her, so I can be rude as well,* which is very hurtful. As a caregiver, you get used to being a soundboard in the patient's line of fire no matter what their mood, but I was not gonna lie. It still was hard, but I was like a brick wall, strong for all. No worries! I'm putting this in my book because to those of you reading who are caregivers, you need this reminder—that you are the one that take all the heat from it all and have to learn to be strong. When you leave the room, then you can let your emotions go. I say this because I am the type of person who did not like to show my emotions in front of Robert as he was trying to heal since he had so many things he was trying to accomplish. Why have him worry about my feelings? However, there is an instance later in this book where you will see how a similar event plays out!

At *noon*, one of the pulmonologists came by—Dr. S—to see Robert, and she answered our questions.

In the interim, I went to the hospital's chapel today. It was very relaxing and comforting. I opened the Bible provided and read verses from Isaiah and Matthew. Thank you, Lord, for the comfort and peace you gave me during this very difficult time.

At *1:00 p.m.*, when Robert stood up for a walk today, he became very dizzy and said he had an awful left leg cramp. His blood pressure was 77/46, his heartrate was seventy-seven beats per minute, and his O_2 was 96 percent (there was never a problem with his O_2!).

They had Robert lie in bed with his legs up and gave an extra drip of medicine for his blood pressure and a muscle relaxer. He was like this until *6:00 p.m.*

In the picture below, it's evident Robert was fed up today:

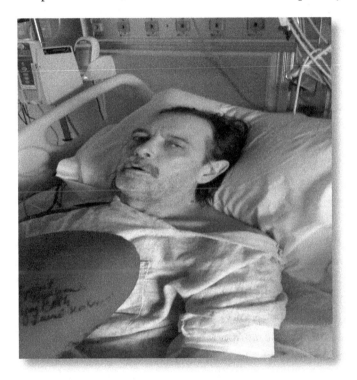

At *7:00 p.m.*, Robert was then able to sit up to eat a little, but his leg pain was consistent. He was given more muscle relaxers.

By *10:00 p.m.*, Robert was able to get up to use the restroom (the bedside commode). (Maybe this is too much information that people don't really need to know, but it is surprising that he was able to do anything with the pain I remember him being in!)

Day 11
December 19, 2015
Room P562

At *12:30 a.m., 1:30 a.m., and 2:30 a.m.*, Robert was given more pain meds for the leg pain he had. His hemoglobin was low. They told us that they were going to do a transfusion and a CT scan (to check for clotting)! I was a wreck, yes. Just when we thought we were out of the water, something else got thrown into the mix! We headed back to ICU; the step-down was short-lived. We headed to room 562.

At *5:20 a.m.*, Robert was in *extreme* pain. He said, "The lung transplant is nothing compared to this." He kept holding his leg to his chest; he could not put it down. They had given him oxycodone and morphine, but he had not touched it. They gave him Dilaudid, and he was finally able to rest.

And then more fun started at *7:00 a.m.* Robert has a seventeen-centimeter (6.693 inches!) hematoma at his hip, in the upper left leg. We were waiting for surgeons to come talk to us. I could tell you right then that I was pretty scared.

Robert was getting a blood transfusion, and it was going well. It would be maybe another hour to an hour and a half. We were exhausted. Everyone seemed very concerned. It was almost 8:30 a.m., and the transfusion was done. It went very well. I thought of the person who donated blood and how it was able to help Robert in this instance. Thank you, donor!

Meanwhile, at *8:30 a.m.*, a technician came in to do an EKG and echo, and I was not very pleasant. They were trying to get Robert to move so they could do the procedure. I said, "He can't. He has a hematoma. He is in pain!" Robert said, "It's okay, Cherie." I apologized, but it just seemed like things were all coming at the most inopportune times! They had a job to do too!

At **9:00 a.m.**, Robert's morning medications were given! A chest x-ray was done, and they still wanted a CT scan. The day nurse was Tim (this was the only time we had a male nurse; he did a great job!).

An Unknown Angel's Gift

A trauma surgeon came in to discuss this hematoma and spoke to us regarding the options, the blood, and its effect on the nerves. Of course, we had questions. This was a very high-risk surgery and was not always successful. He had done a couple of them on very healthy people with not-good outcomes. Robert and I discussed this and would not want to risk another major surgery when he was already recovering with new lungs!

At *9:15 a.m.*, Dr. S came to visit and showed me the x-ray. There was a pool of blood deep within the tissue inside Robert's hip bone. It was above a kidney and pressed on a nerve. This was not close to the skin; it was deep within the muscle tissue. If there was a bleed in this area, you would not do anything. There was no massive bleeding, so the body would take care of it. He told us, "We will watch his hemoglobin. She is stable, and all his vitals are okay."

Robert's quotes today were "And now for something completely different!" and "*Wow.*" Robert said these a lot during his hospital stay! I went home for a while.

Sleep was not happening, but cuddling with the cat was always pleasant!

Well, I was back at the hospital, and Robert was ready to eat dinner… I said, "*Good job!*" Robert was looped up on pain killers and said, "If you hang out at a hospital long enough, you will get a lung transplant!" Okay, Robert, you were correct.

Our night nurse was Janie. She was great and sociable, and I had let my coworker with the same name know that!

Day 12
December 20, 2015

At *7:00 a.m.*, we both had a pretty good night's rest for a change! Robert woke up *demanding* breakfast right away. He was really enjoying his coffee and cold cereal. As was I. We had a nice morning breakfast together every day.

What a routine we were getting into here!

Rob even read the paper I got him today!

We had a couple of great nurses today—Stephanie and Dan. Robert rated his pain at a 1 today on a scale of 1 to 10—wow! (That was me saying *wow*, not Robert.)

At *10:30 a.m.*, Robert had to do his usual strong breathing treatments. If anyone stayed in the room, they had to double mask; that was how strong this bacterial medicine was.

On another note, at *noon*, I still had no luck with finding slippers for Robert… He might need a size 14. His poor feet were so swollen. Update to follow in the future.

Here is Robert's face when I talked about shopping today:

An Unknown Angel's Gift

At *2:00 p.m.*, Dad and Claudia came by for a couple of hours. We were both back in bed later and slept for a little while. I awoke, went for a walk to the main lobby for a while, and called two friends and my aunt in Arizona.

From *6:00 p.m. to 7:00 p.m., we had dinner.* I picked up Subway for Robert and myself. The line was pretty long. (We all know how fun that can be.) The hospital meals blew, so when I was not preparing meals for us when I went home, it was always nice to get us carryout.

By *8:00 p.m.*, Robert and I were watching hockey. Nurse Aron was on the night shift. He was pretty cool. I left awhile during his breathing treatment again. I returned, and Robert said, "Don't sit down yet!"

They came by and said his potassium was too high. I knew that look of concern Robert had, which was not very often. Actually, I thought it is more of aggravation at this point.

Here is a picture depicting this:

At *2:00 a.m.*, they pushed meds to help with the potassium issue. No water intake was allowed.

From *2:40 a.m. to 4:00 a.m.*, numerous nurses tried to remove the old IV line and add a new one. Poor Robert. He was so exhausted and uncomfortable. Me, well, I was a rock star and his rock. We got rest the night before last, so we knew that wouldn't happen two nights in a row. Anyone who is hospitalized knows this rings true. You grin and bear it. Four different medications were pushed for the potassium issue. He also had A-fib issues they were trying to correct. Well, today had made Robert very irritable, understandably so!

Here is me at the same time:

We were both just so thrilled. Today there was a whole lot of information to take in. *Wow!*

An Unknown Angel's Gift

Day 13
December 21, 2015
Room P518

"Let's get you all cleaned up," I said to Robert. A nice hot microwaved shower cap for a sponge bath—oh, what fun. A good relationship makes everything fun. You make the best out of everything. Robert cleaned up pretty well while being hospitalized. And believe me, I got up early to get in the restroom and get cleaned up and made up before the cleaning staff came and before the doctors did their morning rounds. Anyone who knows me knows I do not like to go out without makeup. Side note: I slept in my clothes 90 percent of the time. I didn't want to get too comfortable and then have to be "shipped off" to a different room, a test, or a complication. I was always on my toes, so to speak.

At *7:00 a.m.*, all of Robert's levels looked good. He was up and in the chair, and he had breakfast! It was a good day to get cleaned up; we got one of the hottest nurses during Robert's stay—Nicki—a gorgeous brunette. They came and did an x-ray, and all was good. Robert's first nurse coordinator, Patti, came by today. The surgeon Dr. N came by and let us know that they were placing Robert back on a blood thinner as he was worried about a stroke; there was a 12 percent risk if Robert would be on nothing. Guess what, he could have water again also!

At *9:00 a.m.*, the nurse practitioner Patti came by and discussed things with us. She was awesome. On a personal note, she said she could relate as her husband was hospitalized recently also.

From *10:00 a.m. to 5:00 p.m.*, I was gone and would bring dinner back!

I was back, and we had Chad as Robert's night nurse. He was awesome. He was compassionate and thorough. I made a comment about all the hot, attractive female nurses Robert had, and now he was taking over.

At *5:30 p.m.*, Robert went for a good walk today. He was coming along. We'd be two weeks out tomorrow.

Here he is returning to his room:

Day 14
December 22, 2015

It was *8:53 a.m.* Good morning! It was two weeks today that Robert (and I) had been in the hospital. What a journey it had been.

He had a healthy color and a great smile, and he was making great progress. Keep up the good work, "*Superman*"!

An Unknown Angel's Gift

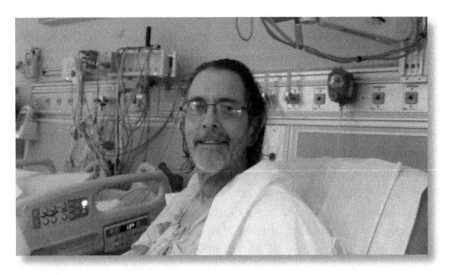

Are you, as the reader, enjoying the play-by-play? You really cannot imagine all that is involved if you have never been through it. Throughout this chapter, you will see where I had taken walks down through hospital or left to go home for day. This is very important for the caregiver to do to keep their sanity. You cannot sit there all day and night, looking at the walls, and be supportive for your loved one if you have not decompressed. This is one of the best pieces of advice I can give you if you are a caregiver reading this. There are so many studies that have been done on stress and its effect on caregivers. It affects you mentally, physically, and emotionally. It also affects your diet (I lost ten to fifteen pounds) and your sleep habits. Take a break. Walk, listen to music, call a friend or family member, go to the gift shop, sit in lobby, or drive home. Of course, your loved one's condition will weigh on your mind nonstop, but to keep your wits, your sanity, and your health in good standing, you must take time for yourself every day. I am proud to say I only had two bad days, and those were in the beginning. When I say *bad (for those of you who know me, I get migraines)*, I had two migraines during Robert's stay. And I was smart enough to realize that it was because I needed to rest more, eat well, and take time to decompress so I would not be crabby, nonfunctional, or unable to hear *all* of what the doctors and nurses had to stay. Plus, you want to be in tip-top shape (*especially*

if you are the primary care giver) to listen to what the staff says and pay attention to what they are administering when they come in at medication time. There were times when there were duplicate medications or something ordered, and I had to ask, "Why is this being dispensed?" If you get the "It's protocol" answer, I still would ask if I were you, "Why is the doctor dispensing this?" Maybe I was a little more protective than usual, but I just could not imagine another complication for Robert.

We were up at *9:00 a.m.* All in all, it was a good night's rest for us. Breakfast? Well… Robert's quote of the day was "They can even fuck up toast." And then the social worker came by. Also, the surgeon Dr. N came by, and since Rob was still in A-fib, he wanted to restart heparin (maybe I mentioned this earlier, or maybe not). Rob's x-ray looked better; the space was getting smaller, so they turned off the suction. Hopefully, there would be no new bleeds anywhere!

At *11:00 a.m.*, I was at home with one of my black cats (decompressing!). I came home and stayed home until 2:00 p.m. today. I made dinner for us tonight and lunch for us tomorrow. (Another piece of advice: If your loved one does not like the food and you like to cook and bake, make an effort to make meals at home and bring back; it will help them gain their strength back quicker also if they are eating foods they like.) Take note that a dietician will be in frequently to talk about food and such. Don't get too worried about this. Just be careful in your selections and watch the salt and sugar, especially if your loved one is diabetic, and if they are not, you do not want them to become diabetic. As you may or may not know, the medications are very hard on the body/kidneys, and you do not want to increase issues with the kidneys.

An Unknown Angel's Gift

And the busy day continued.

At *2:30 p.m.*, the new hospital case manager came by as well as two doctors from the urology and respiratory departments.

At *3:30 p.m.*, Robert went for a fifty-foot walk today, and he said it was so nice to walk without a cannula!

Sometime after 5:00 p.m., the fun started. We were headed to a step-down unit again: room P518! It was a corner room for all to see ya! Okay, first, there was nurse that we did not (absolutely not) want. For one, she had his history incorrect, and Robert and I were very irritated and nervous about the care here in this unit (especially since we had the give the nurse the lowdown)! There was no one at the desk, the blinds were broken, the TV didn't work, and it said we had to pay for it now. And Robert's alarms for IVs keep going off Hello… where was everyone? And we couldn't get to the restroom because the chair sat dead in front of it.

Needless to say, we got a better nurse and a better room down the hall, across from the desk and the fridge (to hold our food). They were good to us. They would even heat the food for us at dinnertime! Robert voiced his concerns to the primary pulmonologist, saying, "Are you trying to get rid of me, putting me in this room that is like a closet," and then he mentioned all of the things above that were wrong. She was hot on it and got him moved to a better, larger room, which he was in for the duration of his stay!

Day 15
December 23, 2015

We were now in room 516. We had a great male nurse who was a former drill sergeant.

At *5:30 a.m.*, the nurse walked in, and Robert sat up before he turned the light on and said to him, "Morning, sir! Yes, sir!" Robert was relaxed; his blood pressure was 97/57. It was very amusing, and the nurse enjoyed it also. He noted that Robert's alarm on the IV pole was not working!

At *7:30 a.m.*, a new nurse named Michella came in. She was very nice and very thorough.

At *9:00 a.m.* today, we were able to get Rob cleaned up quite well—a successful sponge bath as husband and wife. Robert pedaled the pedal exerciser for ten minutes! I stepped out for a while, the pulmonary therapist came by, and Robert walked to the ICU and back!

At *10:00 a.m.*, I had gone home to make Robert his favorite meal: roast beef! I also baked him some brownies!

I stopped by a coworker's as per her request (Diane), and she made us a stuffed cabbage meal.

At *5:00 p.m.*, I made it back before dark as usual. It was like NASCAR on the boulevard, getting back here before dark. I did not want to be on the boulevard at dark or late in the day, and I wanted to be parked and back safe inside the hospital before it got late!

We enjoyed the dinner together. And then he asked me to sit on the bed with him. All was well. We did the bills and had a really nice talk—quality time together. They said he had elevated CO_2 levels, but all was okay now. We zonked out between ten and eleven o'clock at night! No pictures were taken today, but I saved this one for some reason. As the holidays approached, here we were…at the hospital… Robert was progressing nicely.

An Unknown Angel's Gift

Day 16
December 24, 2015
Christmas Eve

Robert jumped right up today with a spring in his step. However, the bed was too low, and he didn't have his bearings. Then he was just fine. It was just a little scare. He was transitioning between the bed and the commode on his own back and forth, getting in and out of bed pretty well once he figured out what worked best for him. His blood pressure was 102/57. Easy-peasy. He has got this. As for me, I was still not sure how well I was handling things. It was all so much to comprehend! But just look at this great pic!

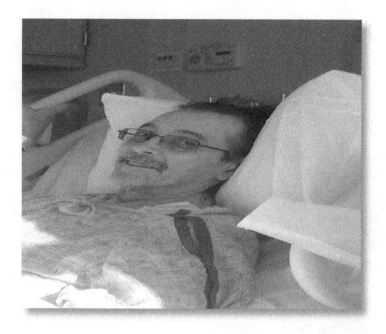

Late in the morning, the occupational therapist came by, and Robert is walking with a walker, no wheelchair in front of him.

Sometime after noon, we were informed that Robert's x-rays looked good that and three (of four) chest tubes were coming out today! By *1:00 p.m.*, the tubes were out!

At around *2:00 p.m.*, Dad and Claudia came by. It was Christmas Eve, so it was so nice to get visitors. And they brought us a present.

Merry Christmas Eve…
The best visitors ever.

An Unknown Angel's Gift

A really nice winter scarf—this gift was for Robert.

It was a really nice visit from the two best parents ever!

Robert's oldest brother came by today also and got a really nice gift plaque box that read "You know all those things you've always wanted to do? Go do them." It was a really nice gift.

After two of the nicest visits from very special people in our life, Robert went for another walk. He took five steps and had some drainage from the remaining chest tube area. Mary (the best nurse practitioner) reapplied bandage to that area, and Robert was as good as new.

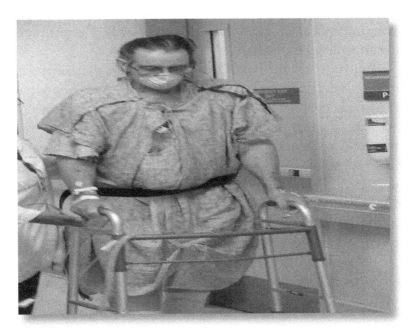

It takes a very strong and dedicated person to take those steps in the right direction of more strength. I watched Robert work really hard at getting well and being stronger. It was scary for me... I knew that in his mind, he was tough and strong enough, but his body was weak. This holds true for anyone in recovery. You have to have the will and the drive to want it. It doesn't happen on its own. You have to be confident and want it. You have to put yourself in the frame of mind of "I got this." Imagine yourself with IVs in your arms and tubes in your body and that you're weak, but you know you have to do this if you want to move on. You learn a lot about a person and life, and you take a long, hard look at yourself in the process. Ask yourself, "How would I do in this situation? Would I be as strong and determined?" This, I tell you: Every patient and every caregiver is different. You have to pull from within. You have to pray. You must have the strength to make it through. There will be days when you feel like you (as a caregiver) can't do it, but then you get this inner peace—this peace and strength that comes from within—and watching your loved one succeed when they work so hard at something fills you with a sense of pride like nothing else. I can tell you I was so proud of Robert and still am to this day. He never complained or showed defeat or weakness. He just pressed forward with determination.

You may hear me repeat myself, but it is important to know that they need you. They may not express it in words or ask for it, but if you know your loved one, just be there for them to listen and give them support. And if they ask something of you, do it nicely and calmly without hesitation. It is all about respect, compromise, and love. The love and respect I feel for this man cannot be put into words. I still wonder to this day, *How did I make it?* But I know in my heart of hearts that viewing his strength made me a stronger person. It made me really look differently at life and all the everyday things we deal with. Life is what you make it.

Robert and I have made this a beautiful life and have turned this situation into something that brought us closer. I thank God every day for the strength I got from within to pile-drive through our days with determination, a sense of grace, a sense of humor, and a strong sense of will to just make it through all the ups and downs that something like this can bring to a relationship. It will not work on its own. Even in turmoil, you have to reach within then recognize and appreciate what you have. In the time we were in the hospital together, we had a lot of quiet quality time to talk and know that a strong foundation existed in this relationship. We were strong when coming into the illness, strong during the illness and recovery, and strong together.

* * * * *

Tonight we had Diane's stuffed cabbage—an absolutely awesome Christmas Eve dinner.

At *7:00 p.m.*, the night shift was about to come on. Then it became *9:00 p.m.* They must be busy. There was no introduction of who the nurse is, there were no blood draws, and there were no meds. By *9:20 p.m.*, Robert's meds were given, and his blood was drawn. His blood pressure was 110/60. Yes, I kept notes of everything, which is evidenced by the play-by-play in this book. Am I keeping your attention? Good!

It was almost Christmas. I was spending the night with my honey in the hospital.

Day 18
December 25, 2015
Christmas Day

Robert was up bright an early, cleaning up. We had another successful spa day!

Me, I did not sleep well for some reason!

After 7:00 a.m., a new nurse named Jen and a nurse assistant named Eva came in. Robert had a lot of drainage from the site of the right chest tube, and they placed fresh, dry dressing again. Robert took some pain meds today, had his breakfast, and was up. He used a walker in the room and to the restroom (minimal assistance). Yea, buddy!

It was *10:00 a.m.* It was also Christmas, and there was no place else I would rather be than with Robert!

An Unknown Angel's Gift

We relaxed and reflected today.

From *2:00 p.m. to 5:00 p.m.*, my brother Tim came by to visit.

All afternoon and evening, Robert talked up a storm with everyone. This was quite a stepping stone for him. Today it was a real pleasure to see him talking so much (*to be able to without getting winded*). That's the ticket. You name it, he talked about it, especially our cars, to everyone. I just sat, beaming, knowing we'd have so much living to do. Nothing would slow us down!

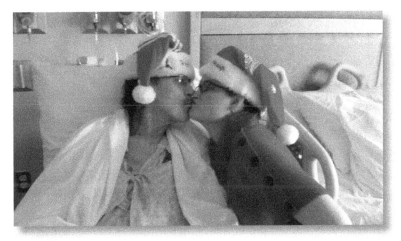

Kiss, kiss, kiss.

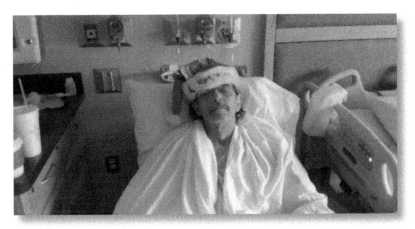

Sweet dreams, love. It was a busy day.

Day 18
December 26, 2015
Day after Christmas

It was *7:30 a.m.* Chen Yu was our nurse, and Nicole was the nurse assistant. Robert was up and at it at *8:30 a.m.*, going to the restroom, and this occurrence was getting regular. That's always something that makes anyone happy!

Late in the morning, we had breakfast, and it was good today.

In the early afternoon, Mike and Lori came up for a visit as well as Jamey.

Late in the afternoon, Robert went for a walk and pedaled the pedal exerciser.

At *7:00 p.m.*, we had a nice mostaccioli dinner. Robert went for a good late-night walk. The goal was three walks per day, and he was on it!

Look at these short, sweet entries. It must have been a good, successful day! And here we are, enjoying one of our favorite past times…hockey!

An Unknown Angel's Gift

Day 19
December 27, 2015

We ate our breakfast, and all of Robert's numbers were really good today. The primary pulmonologist, Dr. A, came by today, and since Robert had not much output from that chest tube now, they would most likely remove it today. They moved us to another private room and told us, "We will have pulmonary therapy come by and get to know all the medications and spirometry. And guess what... you may go home by the end of next week!" Hallelujah for Robert's great progress!

An indications of really good progress was that Robert pedaled the pedal exerciser for thirty-five minutes this morning.

In the morning, Robert took a ten-minute walk and had good vitals after. Today's nurse was Chen Yu, and two nurse's assistants were with him: Nicole and Brittany. They took pride in their work and were just really attentive. This was so great to see—enthusiasm—except... Here's a funny thing. Every time they emptied the urinal, they left it in the bathroom. Ahh, he needed that at the bedside!

In the afternoon, Robert needed a new IV, and he needed someone good because the nurses couldn't seem to do it. They had a male nurse of seventeen years who worked in the cath lab do the IV change. *Bam*...first shot, and he got it! Late in the afternoon, Dad came to visit and stayed with us for a few hours, and we all enjoyed the pie Claudia baked. Delish! Nurse Asha was on tonight. Yea! We liked her. She was very good.

Day 20
December 28, 2015

Lisa (nurse) and Brittany (nurse assistant) were on for the day.

At *8:00 a.m.*, breakfast was over, and all was good yet again! Robert did say that the area where they placed the IV line felt very sore when they flushed it and that since the new one had been placed, it hurt! Again, remember, Robert would not mention anything unless it hurt, and I could see the look on this face when they flushed it. As day went along, it got a little bit better.

Here is his face. Plus, I probably was talking too much, ha:

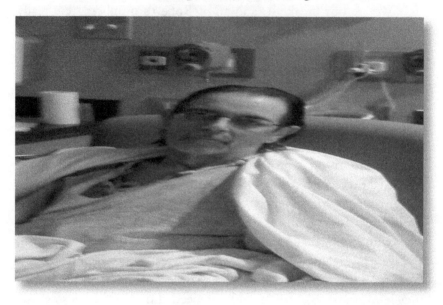

It was *9:00 a.m.* Bad weather was supposed to be approaching today (first time this month). We had been lucky in that respect. By *9:30 a.m.*, they pulled Robert's last tube out! He used the pedal exerciser again, and the occupational therapist came by. Robert was able to walk to the restroom, stand at sink, and clean up. He took a small walk and ate his lunch at around noon.

I was venturing out. I went by the store and our house to prepare tonight's romantic hospital dinner together (chicken, potatoes, and corn)! And I picked up tomorrow's lunch item, snacks, and fruit for us. It was before 5:00 p.m., and well, the roads were ugly while I was getting back to the hospital (I remember traveling east on Highway 96, and it was nothing but ice; I could not see the lane lines). Jesus took the wheel. It took me double the time to get back to the hospital today, but I made it. Robert said he took a ten-minute nap, went for a ten-minute walk, and did his steps on the pedal exerciser! It was a very good day. We had my nicely prepared dinner together.

They were starting Robert on five milligrams of oral Coumadin tonight, weaning him off the heparin.

Day 21
December, 29, 2015)

Today Jen was the nurse, and Brittany was the nurse assistant! Today the surgeon Dr. N, the pulmonologist Dr. S, the fellow Dr. H, and the pharmacist Arin came by. I remember this day well. It was a very informative "pack you with information, hope you remember" kind of day! Dr. Nemeh was very, very pleased with Robert's progress. His voice was sounding much better. I have not mentioned it throughout this chapter, but he was quite hoarse for a while. Dr. N also mentioned that Robert's chest space was filling in as nicely as he had hoped and said that his diaphragm would expand at the bottom. He was just thrilled with Robert's progress. Robert told him at this moment, "I have a lot of living to do!" And the whole staff was smiling along with me, of course!

At 11:30 a.m., we had lunch, and I knew Robert was very appreciative of the snacks and fruit I brought. It was nice to have them on hand.

At around *12:00 p.m.*, well, Robert was given a double dose of magnesium...

At *2:30 p.m.*, his stomach was very upset. You know what happens—no need to explain.

Late in the afternoon, Robert appeared much better, and *we took our first walk together through the halls*! I can still remember the sense of pride I felt at Robert's progress and confidence. He had come a long way in strength, and his perseverance was paying off for sure! His blood pressure was 151/82 after our second walk. His O_2 was at 98 percent, and his heart rate was ninety-six beats per minute.

Eleanor (nurse) and Zak (nurse assistant) came on in the evening. They were two of our favorites. The hospital had what they called a Daisy Award survey. You could fill it out with comments talking about someone who shows exemplary service to their patients, and I nominated these two because they were deserving!

The housekeeping staff at Henry Ford was spot-on. Today a woman had a severe eye issue/infection. I stressed to her the importance of having it looked at, and she was very grateful as she did not realize how severe it could become. I was glad I could offer some input.

And here we are with late-night laughs before shut-eye.

An Unknown Angel's Gift

Day 22
December 30, 2015

Jody (nurse) and Victorus (nurse assistant) were on today.

At *7:00 a.m.*, we had breakfast, which was all good, and we got Robert's hair washed.

A milestone happened today: Robert put his socks on by himself! However, he stated that he was having some pain today. I knew he was pushing himself. Tylenol was not touching the pain today. The portable monitor was removed.

At *8:15 a.m.*, oxycodone was given today, and that helped him tremendously. I would be flat on the floor.

At *9:00 a.m.*, my brother Bill and my nephew Scott came to visit today. It was a very nice visit. Robert and I enjoyed it.

At *11:00 a.m.*, we had a family meeting (my brain was overloaded). This was a discussion on medications and aftercare. Dad, Claudia, Mike, and Jamey came for this as well. This was a two-and-a-half-hour meeting. Like I said, my brain was overloaded, but the meeting was very informative. Everything you could think of involving Robert's discharge was discussed, and the main focus was on medicine and aftercare at home. Labs and medication are big parts of post-op care.

At *1:00 p.m.*, I left for a while. Jamey stayed to visit with Rob, and they went for a walk. I was so glad Jamey and Robert's brothers as well as my dad could be there for him to have some men to talk to and get that added support.

At *5:00 p.m.*, I was back at the hospital, folks! Hahaha. What did I miss? Not a thing. He was in good hands and made leaps and bounds in the last few days! I was so proud of him!

At *7:00 p.m.*, the night shift came on. We had Khalid (nurse) and Ashley (nurse assistant). All was well. It was a good night.

I took no pictures today! The next day was New Year's Eve. We shall see what I pondered up!

Day 23
December 31, 2015

It was *4:30 a.m.* Today was crabby day for Robert. Well, he was entitled to have one on occasion. Surprisingly, he had many more better days. I was lucky as many just whined all the time! Here's something to improve a man's mood: standing and peeing on their own today. Yea! And his Coumadin level (INR) was good today.

At *8:00 a.m.*, Robert had breakfast and was feeling well. Tiffany (nurse) and Nicole (nurse's assistant) were on today.

At *9:00 a.m.*, they took Robert for an x-ray, and I just sat here in the room and thought. While Robert was gone, the unit nurse Diane came in and talked to me. Talk about someone who goes above and beyond their job. She told me to stay positive. We shared a lot and had a very deep conversation. I believe God brought her into the room to see me that day and help my spirits.

Every day, God brings someone near you for a reason. They have a message. Take time to listen and learn from it. Don't take anything for granted. Each day is a gift!

She really made me feel better about the day ahead and life itself.

Here it was, New Year's Eve. We were in the hospital, just moving along, doing what we were supposed to one day at a time. That was all we could do!

At *11:30 a.m.*, Robert and I had lunch together and it was nice.

In the late afternoon, we had a blast from the past. Mike B called today. He was a wonderful, kind soul that we had the pleasure of meeting early in the process. He was just a positive soul with so much encouragement. What a blessing it had been to know him in our lives.

Today we had a screaming, irate patient on the floor. Oh, joy! Those poor nurses! There was crazy, loud action on the floor for New Year's Eve.

Dinner time. All I journaled was that we had dinner together. Meal entries? Not too many details on that!

An Unknown Angel's Gift

As we rang in the New Year together here at Henry Ford Hospital, we couldn't help but be thankful. We were both teary-eyed. We had been blessed. The nurses brought us hot cocoa (with marshmallows)! We put our Red Wing hats on, shared some kisses, watched the ball drop, and fell asleep, feeling grateful… We were grateful for the gift in December 2015 and were looking forward to creating happy, healthy new memories together with fresh oxygen in those beautiful gifted lungs! Thank you, donor. Good night, all. Family, friends, all of our support system, all the staff, thank you for taking such good care of us. See you in 2016!

Right before the New Year. Robert doing his breathing treatment.

Day 24
January 1, 2016

No pics were taken on January 1, 2, or 3. How about that?
It was *6:00 a.m.* Today started off interesting. The restroom breaks were all normal! There were bandage changes. Upon one of the nurses coming in today, I mentioned the red spots along Robert's left leg/upper thigh area. I was very concerned about this, so I wanted to ask. Well, Robert got very angry with me. This was the first time a nurse yelled (snapped) at him. "She's your wife!" (he is not happy

with me), (yes, I said that already), and the nurse said to me thank you very much for mentioning this. She told Robert loved ones ask questions because they care. "I remember some words from an acquaintance of ours "If equals ask!" The Doctor checked the leg and confirmed it is just edema, but glad that it was mentioned. Robert's arms are swollen today also and the nurse suggested he elevate them more.

At *10:00 a.m.*, I went home for the day to cook and bake—therapy.

At *4:00 or 5:00 p.m.* was the usual. Robert states his chest incision very uncomfortable today. He said he did a lot today. After dinner we took a nice walk through the halls together.

Then it was *bedtime*. It was *hard to say what time it was. I actually didn't mark a time.* Asha and Nicole were on for the night shift. We slept well.

Day 25
January 2, 2016

Today Robert told me he woke up in a funk, feeling kind of depressed. It was the first time with this feeling… Well, I gave him a pep talk, and I think it worked. He never worried or said he was not feeling up to par! We both slept well. It must have been the Krispy Kremes and hot cocoa before bed!

Sometime after 9:00 a.m., a new respiratory therapist came by and explained the spirometry breathing machine to us better today. It was much more understandable; we didn't feel like we were in a college class this time!

The nurse practitioner Mary came by, and all was well. Robert had come so far. Dr. S came by as well. "Robert's creatinine kidney levels are a little elevated/borderline," she said. She wanted to watch this and his leg swelling. She would discontinue two of the medications, and they would be doing an echo. Dad called us and, as always, cheered us up! As per the doctor, if the leg swelling would get better, they might send Robert home on Monday or Tuesday next week!

Our afternoon visitor today was Mike B! This gentleman was a huge inspiration and still is to us. He was the most optimistic, enthusiastic person I have ever met. We have not seen or talked to him in months and he came by and visited for two hours (for him to take time out of his busy life to come by really meant a lot to us!) I made sure to let everyone know who has been a major part of our journey we finally got the call!

Nephrology came by. So far, so good. They reminded us that the antirejection medications could really affect the kidneys. Eleanor (nurse) was on now. She was a fabulous nurse. They discontinued two of Robert's medications, and I made a notation. Thank you, God. In only this short amount of time, between the two of us, we could tell when something was added, adjusted, or removed by how much better Robert feels! It made me happy to see him happy!

In closing out this day, I made a note in the journal: "Robert thanked me for talking to him today! It feels good to get recognition from the patient, the man, the one and only!"

Day 26
January 3, 2016

It was *6:00 a.m.* My god, it was early… *Mr. Blackwell, it's time for your Prilosec. Okay, get on with it, ladies.* Lisa and Victoria were on today. They were awesome. This can go unsaid, but I have to mention it. Like any of you know who any of these people are. When you have good care, you remember them well. When I type a name from the time we stayed there, I can remember their faces, their care, and any little extra steps they made to make our stay more comfortable! So thank you to all the fabulous nurses, not just ours but those all over the world! You make all the difference in a patient's stay and their caregiver's experience. Having personality makes all the difference.

To quote Robert this morning, "Great Picasso bowel movement today!" That is just to make you all laugh as you read the detail-for-detail play-by-play days of fun we had.

At *9:00 a.m.*, Robert went for an echo today with and without contrast. Throughout this whole process, they watched his heart closely and kept an eye out for any leg swelling and the creatinine levels. They injected dye to view the heart with and without, and all went well. I took some pics, but since the echo technician was not really thrilled with my doing this, you won't get to see Robert's beautiful heart. Trust me, it's a good one. They still wanted to give Robert Lasix even after stopping the other two medications. Nephrology came by again, and Robert's creatinine was much better now—1.46. They started Robert on an antibiotic today, saying that transplant patients needed it. As you know, I ask about everything being dispensed and what they are for.

On another note, they said Robert and I were like the leads in a romantic comedy. It's nice when you can leave an impression on people you barely know. They could see the love between us, and there was no doubting the care. Obviously, if you can stay by your spouse's side before, during, and after this process, kudos to you. It takes a lot of strength, patience, acceptance, and sacrifice from both parties. I say this to you because if you have not been through it and find out your spouse is ill, and you are about to embark on a long journey like us, you need to know each other well, support each other, communicate, and laugh. Just laugh. You must, or you will not make it. Respect each other's needs, know when to say when, know what to say and when to say it. Smile often. Laugh much. Tell them how proud you are of them. Encouragement goes a long way. Have you even been around a patient, someone you know or don't know? The medications alone can mess with their thoughts. They have much time to think while lying in a hospital bed, as do you. You have to sympathize. You should talk to each other not at each other. It brings you closer, and you'll grow as a couple. You will not only grow as a couple but also as a person. Everything that you witness each day makes you grow as a person.

An Unknown Angel's Gift

Day 27
January 4, 2016

Wow, we were at week 4! Chen Yu and Jody were our day nurses today. Again, they were a couple of the best ones Robert had. There was a cover story on the *Detroit Free Press* today on one of our longtime transplant acquaintances—Pam P. She was a true inspiration to all who met her and knew her. There was also a pic of the transplant group.

Robert was in good spirits today. I took this picture when Robert did not know it. I would always catch him deep in thought. And I thought he looked quite well/healthy today. I wondered if he was thinking of all the "honey to-do-list items" I would have waiting for him!

Thank you, donor. Without you, seeing Robert sitting up and breathing on his own would not be possible. Your selfless gift saved his life, and he has much to think about and accomplish.

Hey, it was snowing in Detroit, Michigan. It looked pretty as I was watching it fall. I wanted us to go home and watch it from the house, not the hospital. You all know what that is like!

It was bath time, hahaha. This was quite the bonding experience for a husband and wife at the hospital. Let me help you!

Dr. S (a new fellow) and the nurse practitioner Mary came by today. They stopped Robert's Lopressor today and IV Lasix. His water retention was improving! That is always a great thing, so keep that in mind when you are in recovery in the hospital: get rid of that water; the sooner the better. Robert's CT scan looked good; only some fluid was seen!

Robert was lightheaded when standing today, but his vitals were okay. His blood pressure was 110/73! It was a relatively quiet day after all the morning excitement. You get very used to the routine and the times when the nurses and assistants come in your room with early-morning must-dos and doctors' rounds, tests, medications, and mealtimes. And just when you think you will get a quiet moment—*bam*—someone comes in!

At *5:00 p.m.*, Robert and I went for a long walk today; we went all the way to the intensive care unit, where he used to be. We visited a gentleman named John and his wife (who I met at the lung transplant support meeting last month and told Robert about). Robert gave John a nice pep talk. Incidentally, we saw them after the fact, and he was doing very well! We ran into Robert's surgeon in the hallway, and he was all smiles upon seeing how well Robert was doing. And we could not thank him enough!

Later that night, Dad and Claudia called and asked us to go on YouTube to listen to an organ donation song: "The Greatest Gift" by David Crowley. What a beautiful song. Take time out of your busy schedule and look this one up and listen to it. It will bring a tear to your eye. Dad and Claudia always came across things to share with us.

Coumadin—here is a fun medication you may hear about if you have a major surgery. Having to check the levels constantly and the dosage adjustments…it's one thing after another. A scare here, a scar there, and a constant prayer to get you through. Stay positive. Tomorrow is another day!

An Unknown Angel's Gift

Day 28
January 5, 2016

It was *6:00 a.m.* We both slept well last night. One of the main pulmonologists—Dr. A, the surgeon Dr. N, Mary (nurse practitioner), and fellow came by, and everything looked good! We were packing things up, and Robert said we needed to take everything off the table. I said, "We do not need all of that like a hotel. "Why," you may ask yourself, "would you even say anything?" This patient was on Prednisone and was full of emotions, so I just let him do what he wanted. In many instances, you will learn this: just keep your mouth shut and roll with it. How's that for advice on an approaching discharge to go home? You will both be a little anxious and take things wrong. I will admit that I did not like his tone, and you won't like your loved one's either. It brought me to acceptance. Just move along, say okay, and avoid an argument.

Late in the morning, Robert went for an x-ray and returned! And all was well in the love and comedy department.

Ginger the social worker came by, and we all had a great relaxed conversation. She wanted to make sure we were not crazy and were ready to venture home. She told us that the whole transplant team of nurses and doctors got emotional when they heard we were going home! She told us no one knew better than us, and she knew we would not screw it up.

In the *early afternoon*, Robert's heart monitor was removed. And he was thrilled. He talked with his buddy Jamey today, his fellow transplant buddy who was also listed for transplant.

While we were waiting for the physical therapist to come by, Robert took twelve steps up and twelve steps down, determined to be strong and successful! His blood pressure was 137/73, his heart rate was 118 beats per minute before and 136 beats per minute after (wow), and his oxygen level was at 92 percent. Just think—Robert's oxygen level used to fall to the sixties and seventies with exercise, and now it was in the nineties like a normal healthy person's. Again, a shout-out to his donor: thank you!

Well, I did not journal this, but I sure remember this aspect of the discharge. And you should take heed. You will have so many hospital workers coming in to go over so much that your head will be spinning. This was the day I had an anxiety attack. I was completely fine during the whole stay and then discharge day—*bam*. You will be brought a big ole bag of medications and a pharmacist to explain it all. You will be told all about home health care and what you will need (e.g., shower chair, bedside commode, walker, cane, etc.). You will be told about the necessary consistent follow-ups. Here is what I wrote: "Labs needed once weekly once discharged; clinic visits once weekly for four weeks, then every two weeks for a month, then monthly, and then at some point, they will change to every two months."

This is very important. Let me give you a piece of advice. Listen carefully. Take notes. It's not an easy journey, but you can do it! You have to show strength as the caregiver, and if you break down once or twice, it's okay. You're human.

I eventually regained my composure and felt like I had all my eggs in a row, but it took some decompression, stopping and thinking, and getting myself together. It all happened so fast, and I just had to be strong and pull up those big-person undies!

Dad and Jamey were here, and here we were before leaving the hospital! Robert was weak but dressed and ready to roll, and I was so proud of him! Look at that big bag of medicine I talked about earlier!

Jamey, Robert, Cherie and Greg (Dad!)

By 4:00 p.m., we were home from the hospital! Robert mentioned and still mentions every so often how good it was to step outside and take air into his new lungs. He could not do that for so long. I cannot imagine or explain how that must have felt, but I can tell you that the look of happiness on his face was priceless. Thank you, donor. Side note: Robert's legs gave out on him on the porch. This was a very scary thing. He is still weak. Like I said earlier, you get into this mindset, and things are rolling along well. And then *bam*—something happens. You take one step back. But then you work through it, and it's okay, like with anything!

Here's some advice for the caregiver: In my experience, the hardest time for the patient is the morning. There are mood swings, which is expected with the Prednisone and with most all other medications the patient is adjusting to. You will feel like they are very bossy and demanding. Just roll with it. They have a lot to accept and get used to. The highlights of a hospital stay with your loved one are as follows:

- not only their health and well-being but also yours as the caregiver
- your attitude toward the situation and each other (accept and grow from it)
- getting to know your nurses and their shifts (they are the heart of your loved one's care, so ask questions!)
- having meals, sleepovers, and heart-to-heart talks with no media with your loved one (you can learn a lot and laugh a lot)
- hope, perseverance, and compliance (they lead to success)
- playing a little lottery here and there (we won $500 on a scratch-off!)

And here are the key items during the hospital stay:

- food from home (it increases the patient's appetite, and they get to taste things they always enjoyed before their surgery as long as it is healthy and compatible with their current medical condition!)

- soft toilet paper and paper plates
- snacks for you—the caregiver—and water
- a journal to write your thoughts in, your favorite music to listen to during downtime, or a book
- a small bottle of your favorite essential oil for you as the caregiver to smell when you need to decompress
- walks to the chapel or hospital lobby, texts or calls with a friend or family member (it does wonders for the soul to talk to someone; they care about you and often can say something you really need to hear that day!)

Thank you to our great friend Jamey. There are not enough words to express our sincerest thanks.

And to Dad too. These were two key people in Robert's recovery and daily struggles.

An Unknown Angel's Gift

As I focused on our being home now, Robert said, "It hurts, but it is just amazing." As he stepped out of our truck at our home, he just wanted to breathe in the air. Breathe in that air, Robert. Take as much time as you want. It must be an incredible experience. And you deserve it! Thank you to Robert for his patience and compliance. We were about to embark on the home part of it now as well as the adjustment and aftercare involved in that next step.

There are just a few last components to add to the closing of this chapter.

Gratitude, courage, and *faith* are key words. There is so much to be grateful for. You never know what life will hand you. I remember a few different key years before the hospital stay that were so difficult for us—2010, 2013, and 2018—but mainly for Robert. I watched him struggle so much and so often and never complain; even after his hospitalization, I could count on one hand the times he said that something hurt. He had the courage, and he was driven to survive and work hard to be a success.

> *Gratitude* turns what we have into enough, and more. It turns denial into acceptance, chaos into order, confusion into clarity... it makes sense of our past, brings peace for today, and creates a vision for tomorrow.
>
> ~ Melody Beattie
>
> TimeWarpWife.com

Here is a verse from Isaiah 40:31: "They that wait upon the Lord will renew their strength." We waited, we prayed, and he answered.

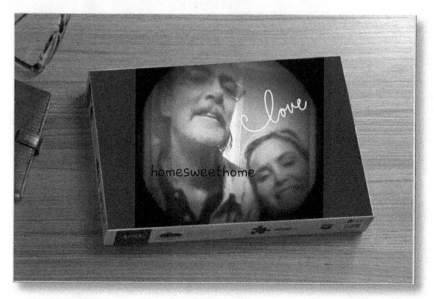

You both got this.

Chapter 11

A Collection of Quotes That Have Been Collected over Many Years, as Well as Some Inspirational Music

This is your life. Do what you love, and do it often.
—Author unknown

I HOPE YOU ENJOY THIS COLLECTION of quotes to inspire you and give you a higher ground over any challenge you may face. Whenever I felt like I could not face the next obstacle, along came a quote or Bible verse at just the right time. I wrote them down; and hopefully, they make you feel enthusiastic and optimistic about facing anything life hands you.

> We are merely moving shadows, and all our busy rushing ends in nothing (Psalm 39:6); all we have to decide is what to do with the time that is given us.

> When you are in a season of challenge, brokenness, and failure, identify the voices that will speak not only to your current situation; we all need accountability, but to your future self. Find people who speak life into where you're going.

Lost time is never found again. (January 2014)

Go confidently in the direction of your dreams; live the life you have imagined. (Henry David Thoreau)

Learn to give flowers while someone is still living; appreciate!

In Christ you have been once far away and are now drawn near.

Ever tried, ever failed, but no matter. Try again, fail again, and fail better. (January 24, 2014)

Forgiveness can't change the past, but it can enlighten the future. Focus on what you can change. The rest will fall into place. (January 25, 2014)

Save more, spend less, and avoid getting ripped off! (January 26, 2014)

Think that today is your day, not tomorrow or next week. For what you want, pray, wake up, and say, "Today." (January 27, 2014)

Kids make you smile and see all that is good in this crazy world. (February 10, 2014)

Set your mind on higher things and make it said.

An Unknown Angel's Gift

Expect good things. Think positive. Get up; say, "Good morning," right at the start; and make it great! (April 6, 2014)

Disappointments are inevitable, but misery is optional. (Joel Olsteen)

Dream. Believe. Accept. Succeed. (May 11, 2014)

We are snared by the words of our mouth (Proverbs 6:2), so say positive things. (June 10, 2014)

Lean not to your own understanding (Proverbs 3:5). Sometimes there is no logical solution. (July 14, 2014) [Here are my added words after the above quote: "You have to just turn your mind off sometimes. If you are constantly trying to figure it out, you will just become frustrated and discouraged."]

Just because you don't see a way doesn't mean that God doesn't have a way. Keep the faith.

He is the potter, and we are the clay.

Respond differently; recognize the tests in your life.

Use opportunities to have a new perspective!

Be generous with your compliments and stingy with your complaints.

> The righteous will flourish like a palm tree. (Psalm 92:12)

> God knows we will face difficulties. Bounce right back. It is only temporary!

> Without hope, one is hopeless. (October 04, 2015)

After 2015, I did not date the quotes.
The following are a collection of quotes I came across on different days while I was at work, "thinking":

> Showing gratitude is one of the simplest yet most powerful things humans can do for one another.

> We must become the change we want to see.

> Smile. Life is chocolaty good.

> You will obtain your goal if you maintain your course.

> You will receive some high prize or award soon.

> Laugh until your heart overflows.

> Facts are stubborn things; whatever may be our wishes, our inclinations dictate our passion.

> God only gives you as much as your cup can hold; everyone's personal cup is a different size!

An Unknown Angel's Gift

When you're riding through the ruts, don't complicate your mind. Flee from hate, mischief, and jealousy.

And this one is very, very good:

Something to do, someone to love, something to live for.

And here are some other quotes I had come across over the years:

of the present time are not worthy to be compared with the glory which I think the sufferings shall be revealed in us.

God and his angels rescue some and schedule others.

Love God, love your neighbors, and, while you are at it, love yourself!

If you don't fight, you don't try.

When you complain, you remain.

When you praise, you are raised.

The Lord is watching over us.

After writing those last three quotes above, we got the long-awaited call the very next day.
And yet more and more quotes to represent life and the power of having a positive attitude not just in waiting or wanting something but after your prayers are answered.

Cherie S. Blackwell

Hope is faith holding out its hand.

Faith is the evidence of things not seen.

We are our own griefs, our own happiness, and our own enemy. Don't let your mind play tricks on you. Life is all that you make it.

And the Best one of all is "Stop existing and start living"!
Thought I would mention a few songs that really say a lot.
This song by Aerosmith—"I Don't Want to Miss a Thing"—is one I listened to every night while lying on the sofa in the hospital room, watching Robert sleep when I couldn't. And the first verse literally gets me every time even until this day because not only was I hearing Robert breathe but also seeing and watching Robert breathe was a gift.

> I could stay awake just to hear you breathing
> Watch you smile while you are sleeping
> While you're far away and dreaming
>
> I could spend my life in this sweet surrender
> I could stay lost in this moment forever
> Ooh, every moment spent with you is a moment
>   I treasure
>
> Don't want to close my eyes
> I don't want to fall asleep
> 'Cause I'd miss you, baby
> And I don't want to miss a thing
>
> 'Cause even when I dream of you
> The sweetest dream will never do
> I'd still miss you, baby
> And I don't want to miss a thing

An Unknown Angel's Gift

Lying close to you, feeling your heart beating
And I'm wondering what you're dreaming
Wondering if it's me you're seeing

Then I kiss your eyes
And thank God we're together
And I just want to stay with you in this moment
    forever
Forever and ever

I don't want to close my eyes
I don't want to fall asleep
'Cause I'd miss you, baby
And I don't want to miss a thing

'Cause even when I dream of you
The sweetest dream will never do
I'd still miss you, baby
And I don't want to miss a thing

And I don't want to miss one smile
I don't want to miss one kiss
Well, I just want to be with you, right here with
    you
Just like this

I just want to hold you close
I feel your heart so close to mine
And just stay here in this moment
For all the rest of time
Yeah, yeah, yeah, yeah, yeah

Don't want to close my eyes
Don't want to fall asleep
'Cause I'd miss you, baby

And I don't want to miss a thing

'Cause even when I dream of you
The sweetest dream will never do
I'd still miss you, baby
And I don't want to miss a thing

I don't want to close my eyes
I don't want to fall asleep
'Cause I'd miss you, baby
And I don't want to miss a thing

'Cause even when I dream of you
The sweetest dream will never do
I'd still miss you, baby
And I don't want to miss a thing

Don't want to close my eyes
I don't want to fall asleep, yeah
I don't want to miss a thing!

"Hallelujah" is a good one as well by Leonard Cohen; both Robert and I love it as well.

    Now I've heard there was a secret chord
    That David played, and it pleased the Lord
    But you don't really care for music, do you?
    It goes like this, the fourth, the fifth
    The minor falls, the major lifts
    The baffled king composing Hallelujah

    Hallelujah, Hallelujah
    Hallelujah, Hallelujah

    Your faith was strong, but you needed proof

An Unknown Angel's Gift

You saw her bathing on the roof
Her beauty and the moonlight overthrew her
She tied you to a kitchen chair
And she broke your throne, and she cut your hair
And from your lips she drew the Hallelujah

Hallelujah, Hallelujah
Hallelujah, Hallelujah

The song "Maybe I'm Amazed" by Jamie Dornan is also an amazing portrayal of this love.

Well, maybe there's a God above
As for me, all I've ever learned from love
Is how to shoot somebody who outdrew you
But it's not a crime that you're here tonight
It's not some pilgrim who claims to have seen the
     light
No, it's a cold and it's a very broken Hallelujah

Hallelujah, Hallelujah
Hallelujah, Hallelujah

Hallelujah, Hallelujah
Hallelujah, Hallelujah

Well, people, I've been here before
I know this room, and I've walked this floor
You see, I used to live alone before I knew you
And I've seen your flag on the marble arch
But listen, love, love is not some kind of victory
     march, no
It's a cold and it's a broken Hallelujah
Hallelujah, Hallelujah
Hallelujah, Hallelujah

There was a time you let me know
What's really going on below
But now you never show it to me, do you?
But remember when I moved in you
And the holy dove, she was moving too
And every single breath we drew was Hallelujah

Hallelujah, Hallelujah
Hallelujah, Hallelujah

Now I've done my best, I know it wasn't much
I couldn't feel, so I tried to touch
I've told the truth, I didn't come here to London
    just to fool you
And even though it all went wrong
I'll stand right here before the Lord of song
With nothing, nothing on my tongue but
    Hallelujah

Hallelujah, Hallelujah
Hallelujah, Hallelujah

Hallelujah, Hallelujah
Hallelujah, Hallelujah

Hallelujah

    There are so many more I could list, but anyone who has been or is in love or has been through so many life journeys knows that music is healing. And I couldn't have made it through my days without it as well as my faith, friends, and family.

An Unknown Angel's Gift

This poem by Richard A. Carloy says it best—that you may be your best:

> Let Gratitude Be Your Attitude
> Every day of your Life is a gift from God
> Don't squander it
> Don't waste it by being angry with anyone
> Don't let it slip away by feeling sorry for yourself
> Be grateful for this precious "gift of life" and spend it
> By being as happy and as thankful as you possibly can.
> Let your mind dwell on the good things which have happened to you.
> Let gratitude be your Attitude.
> Think of your assets, and don't let anyone else spoil your day for you.
> Enjoy EVERY day of your life to the fullest.
> Realize that you can add to the joy of each day by making someone else happy.

Anyone who knows me knows how optimistic and enthusiastic I am. I love life. I love to dream. I love to live. I enjoy being around people who make me laugh and I enjoy making them laugh in return. I am blessed with a wonderful man in my life, wonderful family and wonderful friends. I believe wholeheartedly each day is what you make it. You have to grab it and make every moment count. As it says above each day is a gift from God truly. If you are blessed with wonderful people in your life let them know as often as possible how special they are and just "live". Enjoy life. "Breathe" in all the possibilities and chase your dreams. No matter how long it takes don't ever give up. There are so many reasons to be happy and grateful and make each day count!

Cherie S. Blackwell

And here are three closing quotes:

> Imperfection is beauty, madness is genius, and it's better to be absolutely ridiculous than absolutely boring. (Marilyn Monroe)

> And keep smiling because life is a beautiful thing and there's so much to smile about! (Marilyn Monroe)

> Everybody should be quiet near a little stream and listen. (Author unknown)

Chapter 12

He's Home!

Adjustments to Our Health, Attitudes, and Well-Being—the Dynamics of It All and then Living Life All It Is Supposed to Be: A Long Time Coming With Many Shared Photos of the Instrumental Family and Friends in Our Life

When you riding through the ruts, don't complicate your mind.... Don't bury your thoughts; put your vision to reality.
—Bob Marley, "Wake Up and Live"

I REMEMBER WHEN THINKING BACK HOW there was one day when he was in the hospital right after the new year, and I drove home to run an errand and get some food to prepare. I stopped at the store and bought an expensive scratch-off. Robert was doing really well that day, and I felt lucky! I thought we only won $50, but little did I know that it was $500. That was the beginning of nothing but good luck for us. As we embarked on this new journey of life outside the hospital setting, we couldn't be happier. Robert was home, and we would have some more hurdles to cross and bumps in the road. But he was out of the hospital. And to see him so excited to breathe in that fresh air filled my heart with joy!

So let's talk about being home now, all the rehabilitation, and just so many more examples of a true hero who wants to do everything he can to be the best he can be and take care of the lungs he was blessed with. Our full social fun calendar will come in time!

* * * * *

To continue his life, Robert would need to take his pills every day. There were about twelve pills a day with a couple of others to be taken as needed. He would continue to do breathing blows into a machine for the rest of his life. Right now, his numbers ranged from the 1.70 to 2.05. (At the end of this book, years into the journey, I will tell you how much those numbers increased [improved].)

The body is an amazing thing. Think of what it adapts to, what you push it to do, how it reacts, and how you react. I believe that if you want something bad enough, it will happen. And I believe that everything happens for a reason. This person's strength that I write about is unbelievable. To watch his determination and strength was quite an inspiration to me. I cannot say it enough. Watching someone you care about struggle and fight makes you a better and stronger person yourself. You see so very many things in life differently.

Here we were on January 6, 2016 (day 29 since the surgery). We were home, safe, and sound, but there was still so much to do to make sure Robert was comfortable and on the right road to recovery. He was physically weak, but he would never admit that. But as you will learn, it didn't take him long to build his muscle and physical strength back up again because he was determined, and that is what patients must have. They must have the strength and determination to grow, learn about their own strengths and weaknesses, win the battle, and become the person they were meant to be to live the life they were meant to live with the new organ they were blessed with.

My dad was here, and he and he brought us milkshakes! Dad and Jamey were working on installing some handrails. They were very much needed, and we were very grateful that they did this for us. Well, I had to run some errands. These things don't do themselves, people. I left and was gone for three hours. Shower seat? Check. Thermometer? Check. Blood pressure cuff? Check. Returns? Check. And lunch for us? Check.

Here he is on his first morning home with his new lungs (January 7, 2016):

Robert was up early. His breakfast was eaten, his meds were taken, his blows were undertaken, and he slept okay (both of us, actually). Robert slept with his mouth open a lot. I think it was because there was so much air to take into those wonderful big healthy lungs. It was the dawn of a new day—a great day, a great adventure. We had a great visiting nurse.

Here we were, still on day 30 since the surgery (January 7, 2016). The visiting nurse visited with us to draw Robert's blood and get the lowdown on the history of Robert's medical condition, the surgery, and our story. I sent the results to the primary care doctor's office (this needs to be done if the patient is on Coumadin) so

Rob's INR levels could be checked to make sure the correct dose was being given (in case you did not know that—fun fact!). And Robert's Prograf levels (this is one of the immunosuppressant drugs Robert would be on for his whole life) needed to be checked weekly until they had his level where it should be. The dosage would be the same once that was determined, and it could take months of lab draws.

Here was a major screwup we had to deal with today. The medical supplier at Henry Ford screwed up Robert's order and did not deliver all the supplies to us with his nebulizer. So I drove to Henry Ford's downtown campus as no one close to here had it. As I walked into their "store," I witnessed in person their rudeness to patients and caregivers. (When Robert talked with them on the phone this morning, they were like "What's your problem?") What place of business treats their customers that way? There was another woman there who was in same boat as me. She did not get all the supplies for her husband as the orders were documented.

Sometimes in this world, you deal with people and situations that make you wonder, and you have to control your anger and come up with a solution.

As I was dealing with this person, they thought they were going to charge me. I said, "You forgot to send us all the requested supplies, and we did not hear back when inquired about it." Needless to say, I kept my cool, and we got the items we needed.

There are so many unexpected stressful situations you will run across in any caregiving process. You have to keep you cool and solve the problem. As I like to say, if you solve the problem, as the caregiver, there will be less stress on the patient, and they can just worry about their recovery and steps they have to take to make it work!

It was day 31 since the surgery (January 8, 2016). It was nice to wake up in bed together. It seemed like years ago since this was possible even though it had only been weeks. Robert slept well. He was using the pedal exerciser. Robert was taking his medication and eating well. And he was able to take his first shower at home today!

It was day 32 since the surgery (January 9, 2016), and it was a really good day. A physical therapist and a pulmonary therapist came

An Unknown Angel's Gift

today, and they were very impressed with Robert, considering what he had been through.

Like I said earlier, it is amazing what the body can do to heal itself, but you *have* to put forth the effort. It does not happen on its own. You have to be compliant with the doctors, nurses, and therapists and listen to your gut. If you have a question, ask. *If* equals call—always. Never assume. That's just a little piece of advice there that a nurse gave us many years ago.

Robert was very happy with his meals and things tasting good. Even though it is a good day, you will still have bumps in the road. It can be a good day, but that doesn't mean it won't come without some obstacles, aches, pains, and questions.

Robert said he had a rough night sleeping. I even noticed his breathing was back to when he was on oxygen. He would breath so hard that the bed would move with each breath. Who else didn't get good rest? Me. But that's okay because I picked up the zs when I could, and it was enough. I was stronger than I thought. When I questioned Robert about his sleeping difficulty in this instance, he said he was more comfortable on his side but had difficulty getting comfortable; he was just restless. I said, "Yes, me too."

It's nice when you can communicate with your loved one before, during, and after the process of whatever type of medical illness/situation that you are presented with. Communication is important in any relationship, but it's especially important when you are going through rehabilitation. If something didn't seem right to Robert, I was on the horn with the nurses, asking questions. And you know what? They will figure it out. That is what they are there for.

It is very scary when you are watching someone recover. You have to give them their space, let them heal, and just be supportive and not overbearing. I like to pride myself in how I wasn't too overbearing in this whole process, just supportive. Robert and I did not get into one disagreement during his hospital stay or once he was home. We were both patient with and supportive of each other. When you love someone, that is how you should treat one another. Yes, we are on aftercare post-surgery book chapter, but sometimes I go into relationship "facts" because we know what it takes to work! So let's get on with the day…

Robert did a lot of sleeping in between his medications, and he worked out also. Yes, that's my superhero. Regardless of if he felt tired or not up to par, he still was compliant and knew what he needed to do to continue to heal.

Here is something I saved during this time:

Here we were at days 33 and 34 (January 10 and 11, 2016). Time just kept flying by. As we watched the days pass, I watched Robert get stronger and stronger, and it made my every day complete! It was pretty exciting to see how well he was progressing. Anyone

An Unknown Angel's Gift

who knew him knew he was tough, and he was one to admire. I am sure I have said this before, but it is worth repeating: He has a big heart, a strong mind, and a strong spirit and would do anything for you. He applies himself. He thinks about something before he does it. These two days I mentioned were more of good days, but there was still restless sleep for the superhero. I think it was just a matter of getting comfortable. His body was still healing and had so many things to adjust to, including the medicines and the workouts. His whole system had to adjust emotionally, physically, and mentally!

Can I just say something? Not a day went by that I didn't look at him sleeping or napping and get emotional and thank God and the donor that he was breathing without oxygen and was healing! I know, I know, too many exclamation points. That just shows my enthusiasm! On another great note, I had a great talk with my dad today. I enjoy talking to our family members. It's everything. It always comes at the right times with the right person. They always give you suggestions, input or a laugh you need and I am forever grateful. Thank you, Dad, for always know what to say not just to me but to Robert too.

On another note, I went to get gas today and fell at the pump. Luckily, I caught myself just right—no major injury. Like you all really need to hear this, but it was icy, I was tired, and I was rushed. I needed to stop and not be in such a hurry, I guess! I came out of the situation with flying colors and just a little foot pain. There's never a dull moment out there in this crazy, rushed world.

It was day 35 since the surgery (January 12, 2016), and Robert and I were at his first follow-up at the hospital since he had been home. Guess what? All his x-rays and blood lab work looked great. They took his many, many stitches and staples out today. The doctors were very pleased with Robert's progress. In one of the doctor's words, he was "extremely pleased." There was still a little fluid in the upper left lung area, but everything should progress along, healing okay with that subsiding. Of note, Robert and I fell asleep in the exam room by the time we got to the last appointment today. *Knock-knock*, it was the surgeon who operated on Robert. We were like "Hello." I was sure we were not the first group of people he had found resting in the exam room. You never mind waiting for the best.

Here is a picture of the seventy-plus staples that were removed from Robert's chest. Can you imagine having to endure that? And the two chest tubes he had on each side that they removed at the hospital before we left? We watched those daily to make sure there were no issues at the site, and it was very stressful. He had great nurses, but that was just one thing during the process that was stressful. This is a quote that I believe helped: "God is the source of our strength."

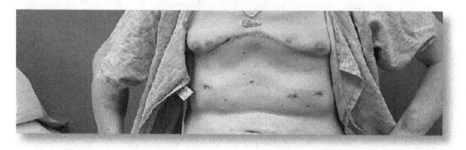

It was day 36, as you know, since the transplant (January 13, 2016). How do you like the play-by-play? Well, it is a story, and it is best told as how it really was.

Today, it was a beautiful day. Waking up cuddling with someone who was too uncomfortable to get any rest a month ago was not an easy task, nor was it easy for the other. If you're asking for words for this day—this moment—it's really indescribable, but I will just say these two things: amazingly romantic and loving. To see your loved one able to rest after so many days and nights of being uncomfortable is a great feeling. However, Robert did wake up at 4:30 a.m. feeling very lightheaded. He was on a high dose of Lasix, and the transplant team said to go back to a lower dose. Robert's blood pressure was 148/93 in the early morning. And much better it became with the lower dose.

On another note, my human resource director phoned me today, saying they wanted to share our story in my work newsletter, and we okayed this. Here is the piece:

ARC Employee's Spouse Receives *the Gift of Life*

Cherie Blackwell has been an ARC employee for 22 years, first working in the Royal Oak and Livonia clinics and now in the Novi offices as part of the Administrative group.

On December 8, 2015 at 9 p.m., she and her husband Robert received a life-saving phone call from the Henry Ford Transplant Center in Detroit, Michigan. Robert, who had been on the waiting list for lungs for over 8 years, was about to undergo transplant surgery. Their suitcases had been packed for the anticipated long hospital stay all of that time, only changing out as the seasons changed, and a call that did not come for them. During this waiting period, she and her husband became very active mentoring others in a support group with the hospital which she said has helped them both keep strong and positive.

Cherie is off from work now helping her husband recover from the surgery that saved his life. But Cherie wanted her "ARC family" to know about this wonderful gift that they are calling the best Christmas Gift ever. There is an article in the January 4, 2016 Detroit Free Press that discusses the transplant program and a picture of Cherie with her father discussing Robert's recovery.

And here we were at day 37 since the surgery (January 14, 2016). I was not quite as motivated as usual, but I did get a lot of sleep. All in all, it was a pretty good day even though Robert was a little down today and quite "snappy." I'd say it was definitely the medication. He didn't realize it, so it was okay. He was under stress while recovering, but he never complained. Even before his surgery, he didn't complain. It was so nice not to be with a complainer or a negative person! The visiting nurse came, and all was just fine.

And here we are at day 38 since the surgery (January 15, 2016). There were breakfast, showers, and better attitudes today! Robert got a phone call from the UAW retiree meeting president today. He wanted to check on him since he had not been at meetings, and they were concerned. They would be giving a talk at February's meeting (Gift of Life) and talking on the importance of organ donation. Here is a fun fact: I had half of December's laundry done and away today. There were more piles of laundry than I had ever seen in our home. I never thought to ask for help with that. I just would grab changes of clothes during the hospital stay.

It was day 39 since the surgery (January 16, 2016). Robert woke up consistently at 4:00 a.m. Every day was like a roller coaster. To any of you reading this who have not had any surgeries, be prepared for restlessness as your body adjusts to the medications, and remember that every person's pain tolerance is different. There will be good days and bad days. It's an emotional and physical roller coaster, and I described it this way many a times at our transplant support meetings. It is not only that way for the patient but the caregiver as well. Just be sure to keep the lines of communication open, and you'll find that to be very helpful! Here is another fun fact since we got home: since we went to the hospital during the holiday season, all of the decorations were up still to this day (this day we are on right now in the book), so I was able to get much of that down and organized!

Day 40 through day 42

What? Three days' logs were written on one page of my journal. They were pretty good days. I would not lie about this! On day 40 after the surgery (January 17, 2016), we slept right through the physical therapist's phone call to our cell phones and the house phone. Wow, that is what you call tired. I ran out to the grocery store. My HR director called from work with a very happy phone notification for us: the doctors I worked for wanted to send us meals. It was a service that had a list of numerous restaurants on a list, and you could choose meals. This was one of the nicest, most thoughtful gifts anyone could give. We were excited to look over the menu. This would save a lot of time from preparing meals during this recovery process!

Day 43 through day 44

What? Two days' logs were written on one page of the journal. Robert saw his primary care doctor today, and he stopped taking the iron. That stuff can really mess with your bowels—just a fun fact there! Don't be afraid during the recovery process, if there are stomach issues, to mention it to your doctor. It very likely—most of the time—that is medication related. They drew blood today. It was nice to get out together and get fresh air even if Robert had to have a doctor's appointment. We headed back to the house right after for lunch, and the physical therapist was expected. Believe it or not, every day was nonstop, but we would make it. I was sure of it.

All of this is not for the faint of heart. You have to be a tough, strong-willed, fierce individual ready to tackle the world. Yes, both the patient and the caregiver must grab the bull by the horns!

Robert told me to take a picture today because I was staring. Well, he shouldn't look so good and healthy like a young marine in his twenties! That's no exaggeration, people.

Here is a healthy pic of Mr. Superman:

Day 45

Where did the time go? Poor Robert battled with frequent bowel issues. Plain and simple, it was hard for his body to adjust to

the medications. I was off to the store for some Imodium and the best teddy bear I could find. I don't care how old you are; a stuffed teddy bear will make you smile from ear to ear, and that it did. I purchased some instant breakfast drinks for him also, and that helped him considerably. I am sharing this because this seemed to help many that I mentioned this to. The medications and the stress can cause stomach issues! Keep Imodium on hand and instant breakfast drinks! And take it one day at a time. I'm not sure how thrilled my husband will be that I shared that little tidbit of his recovery, but this book not only tells our story, but it also offers advice to people, and that piece is huge.

Day 46

I placed one sentence in my journal, and here it is: "Every day is a successful journey!"

Here is a nice pic of Robert resting (relaxing)! There are no pictures of me I could find like this, hahaha:

Day 47

Today was a very good day for Robert. He was able to take his first nap in the bed today. Seeing him comfortable and smiling made my day! And my place of employment sent a very nice meal certificate for us! We had an amazing steak-and-seafood dinner tonight. This was a long time coming.

Day 48

All day today, we were at the hospital, and we were exhausted. And I know you all get it. Anyone who has been through it knows. And that's all I have to say about that!

On day 49, Robert asked me a simple question; however, I did not write the question, just the answer. I said, "Don't ask me something with such simplicity. My life is complicated."

Check this out: in my journal, from day 50 through day 57, there were no entries… It was just that Robert was doing so well. I mean, what a rock star. His lab results, x-rays, blows, blood pressure, and pulmonary rehabilitation—he was just rocking it. I prepared Robert's paperwork today for his hair donation for Wigs for Kids.

Day 58 through day 61

There was just a big happy face in the journal.

Day 62

Robert had to have an echocardiogram. The electrophysiologist recommended an ablation. Robert had some A-fib issues throughout this process. He never did before the surgery, but he did afterward. We stopped and got a Robert a cane, and he was using it well today. We also bought a stethoscope, and I could now listen to those beautiful-sounding lungs!

Day 63

Robert's good friend Jamey picked him up and took him for a haircut. It looked fantastic. I was glad he got to have some time with a friend. It was still hard to believe that over twenty years of long hair was gone.

Day 64

Robert went to his UAW retiree meeting. Gift of Life was there, speaking on this day. This was fantastic. Getting the public educated was so important. Robert's UAW president called him three times to check on him in the last few months, which was really cool. Robert did the dishes today. I didn't think he was going to need me at home much longer!

Day 65

We had four simple words: "Bye-bye, commode seat assistance." To be funny, those things are a pain in the ass to have in your bathroom, and they take up a lot of room. Our nephew Mike visited today too.

Day 66

Robert was a little congested. We hoped this was nothing. Our nephew Scott called to check on him, which was pretty cool.

Day 67

I was quite concerned. Robert had heavy wheezing and chest congestion in the evening.

Day 68

Now it was the morning, and Robert had continued to cough and sounded quite bad. This may sound gross, but he coughed up a large sputum and felt much better. They teach you in the hospital as the patient after these things to cough, cough, cough, and get that junk out if need be! But we were still a wreck, wondering if he may need to be hospitalized.

Day 69

Guess what? All was good, and there was a happy face or two!

Day 70

I was back to work. No comment!

Day 71

We headed downtown for Robert's ablation. You remember that procedure I mentioned earlier in the chapter? Yes, he was going to have it done. The procedure went very well, as the doctor had expected. I contacted everyone in family to let them know. I took a walk to the other end of the hospital. Robert's room for the night was not busy at all; not many patients were in this wing at all. He was in room F346. If any of you know that floor at Henry Ford Hospital, You know it's a nice, cozy little area. I had an adjoining room where they let me stay the night with a reclinerlike pullout bed—not too shabby. Of note, I did have a migraine on both days, but my Imitrex did the trick!

Day 72

We came home. Robert was exhausted again. I was so emotionally drained. We stopped by the pet store, and I drove over a parking block. I felt like a real idiot. I was so hard on myself so many times.

Day 73

It was a new day! I was feeling fresh, positive, and optimistic. It's amazing what a good night's sleep in your own bed can do. Thank you, God. Thank goodness for medications for headaches and hormones—a little humor there for the women out there. I know you get it. I was on a really great high for the day. Robert and I took a walk today. I can still remember it now. It was 63 degrees in February in Michigan. And my husband could breathe in that air, breathe it out, hold my hand, and walk with me without getting winded. Did I say, "Thank you, God"? Yes, I did. Let me say, "Thank you, donor." I would never tire of looking at Robert and seeing him breathe so easily without struggling. That was my daily dose of happiness and gratefulness. I had no complaints.

Day 74 through day 77

Robert continued to improve, and I continued to get back to normalcy in the work schedule/routine. Robert wanted to snow-blow so bad. No…not yet, Robert! That had been on his list of things he wanted to do with those new lungs!

Day 78 through day 80

Robert was getting stronger and stronger. We took the shower seat apart. He had enough of sit-down showers, I suppose! It was nice to see the commode and shower seats gone. It was a sign of recovery. He was walking on the treadmill. Thank you, God. He was feeling better and better every day.

As I continue to write this book, I sit here with tears in my eyes as I relive each and every moment. You have to understand the day-by-day struggles and the many things that people take for granted. I can't imagine doing what Robert did. He is a true superhero. Watching the improvement was incredible. His emotional and physical struggles, I am sure, were tough, but remember when I said

Robert doesn't complain? He does not. Even after we were home, throughout all of these days, he did not complain. He took everything in stride and made it work! And I was more proud as each day passed!

Day 81 through day 90

Robert was doing well. But did you expect anything less? His labs continued to be good, and there was no change in medications!

Day 91

Robert returned to pulmonary physical therapy!

Day 92 through day 93

Robert was sore. He said he overdid it at the pulmonary physical therapy workout! He was so happy to be able to go out and even just walk around the house and the yard without getting winded. Can you imagine how good that feels to someone who struggled for eight years with every single task, even sleeping, with an oxygen hose? He is proof that you can be successful if you work hard and be compliant. He is the perfect poster child of success for a transplant patient.

Day 92 through day100

Robert's primary pulmonologist recommended a sleep study at his visit as many A-fib patients can get sleep apnea. We spoke to Robert's electrophysiologist, and they were in agreeance. It was a good idea. So he did wear the apparatus at home and awaited the results. In the meantime, Robert had been having back pain for the last two weeks on and off and went for a back x-ray and ultrasound, as per his medical doctor. They would also do some labs. His INR number was okay, and his dosage was to be kept same as well as his other medications. Everything turned out okay. He was back in full force at pulmonary and physical therapy.

You will find that sometimes, when you are the patient and even the caregiver, you'll push yourself because you want things to be as you want them to be, with nothing slowing you down. A nurse pointed out a good fact one day. She said that for every day your body is in bed, that is a month of muscle recovery or more.

Day 100 onward

Well, after day 100, I stopped marking the days in my journal. You will note that I did not place dates either. The days go by so quickly. Each day is a test, however. You are busy. You are tired. You are emotional. You have to roll with it and communicate. We were both pretty snappy at each other, and I found it was because it was cold out, and we had cabin fever.

Wait, here it is. I noted day 110 in my journal. I baked us some cookies, and that made us happy. Ha. They stopped one of Robert's medications but added another one and moved the Lasix to every other day. We were sure that the Prednisone was affecting Robert's moods also, and they added another immunosuppressant this week, which meant, yes, bowel and sleep issues.

The doctors informed us that Robert needed to see a dermatologist as they worried about transplant patients developing skin cancer. Well, okay, anything they said, he would do.

You see, every time you get comfortable, they throw another item your way. A wrench into the "just when you were feeling comfortable" time is what I call it. Just when you think everything's going smoothly, there comes a nice little bump in the road—another appointment to add to your list.

At any rate, as long as Robert was feeling fine, it did not matter to me. We would do everything we needed to do to make sure there were no issues.

An Unknown Angel's Gift

Ten days had passed, and there were still no journal entries. Robert was four months out already from his transplant! Life was moving along quickly, and we took nothing for granted.

Today was a beautiful day. I got to see something I waited a very long time to see. Robert drove the GTO muscle car with no oxygen, shifting through all the gears and not becoming exhausted or winded. Life is beautiful, and that is one of the many wonderful things Robert can do now…living life. We waited so long, and I could not wait to see him enjoy this moment. He commented on how very nice it was. And here is a picture of that very moment.

As we move forward in this chapter, I would like to share many moments we cherished and were able to enjoy since Robert got his gift, and he's moving along nicely day by day.

Onward we go to a very momentous weekend. Robert and I spent a very nice weekend cutting trees. It was so nice to work outside together. And Robert didn't have to stop and catch his breath because he became winded. He had no problem breathing in that fresh air with lungs that improved every day.

We drove both our muscle cars. I don't think you could peel the smiles off our faces. As we continued to live one day at a time, the days flew by so fast, and it sure was nice to spend so much time together with Robert becoming healthier and healthier day by day.

And here is another wonderful moment. These may seem mundane to some, but to us, they are blessings.

As we ventured to a doctor appointment one day, we shared quite a few laughs while at the office. I love this man. And we even took the stairs, not the elevator!

Fifty more days passed. The weather was nice. Life is a gift. We are blessed. We attended some events and parties, and seeing Robert able to enjoy the food, drink, and conversation and us being able to walk together hand in hand, talk, and laugh made my day every day.

On April 2016, Robert washed my mustang, and there was no exhaustion!

All of a sudden, I wrote a day and a date in my journal: day 154, May 11, 2016. We went to our first hospital lung support meeting today. We had been away from it for six-plus months. And of all things, it was a Gift of Life meeting with a donor-family speaker and Gift of Life speaker. Take my word for it. It was a really great meeting that would make you appreciate life even more as you hear the sharing and care. And can I just say how proud I am of Robert and how great he looks and sounds? It's just a miracle from God.

An Unknown Angel's Gift

A couple more weeks passed as we lived life, and the weather in Michigan was just stunning in late May 2016. Robert continued to adjust well; he just had the usual stomach issues as he tried to adjust to medications. We came upon Memorial weekend and enjoyed our cars, our gardens, and BBQ-ing. It was simple. It was wonderful. It was everything. It does not take much to please us in this world. To have our health, happiness, and time together to enjoy the simple things in life are all we need.

As we approached Robert's six-month post-op point, we were at another doctor appointment, and I made a notation worth mentioning: they finally adjusted Robert's medications some more, and most importantly, he did not have to do the breathing treatments anymore! I was confident this would help him.

Here is a pic of Robert on June 10, 2016—six months since the transplant!

There are many things that make me smile in this life. Nightly I lie in bed and just listen to Robert breathe. Does that sound crazy to you? Hear someone you love breathe without difficulty is the greatest gift, and so is seeing him do things without difficulty or getting winded.

We continued to move right along. Robert had no infection and no rejection! That was the best news. Since he had been off CellCept (immunosuppression drug), he was doing much better and had less stomach issues (just mentioning the drug in case any of you posttransplant patients reading this who are on it are having stomach issues; mention it to your doctor, and maybe they can update your medications as well, and you will feel better). The tremors, which were very common, had improved as well, which meant Robert was doing more and more. He was also out and about more and more. It was now dusk, and we went for a ride in the GTO.

Another fifty days passed without journaling. All I can tell you is that during the days I did not journal, we were out in the world, enjoying life. We breathed in each day, smiled, laughed, cruised, ate, drank, and shared our thoughts and dreams. We went to more car shows in the summer of 2016 than we ever had in our whole relationship. Robert looked and felt better than ever. It made me happy beyond words. I can tell you so many play-by-play daily things that I journaled or just my thoughts and joys about this experience; but really, there are not enough words, poetry, or music to explain the joy we experienced as we enjoyed life day by day with this new lease on life we waited so long for. Anyone who knows me knows I love music, all kinds. Here is a good one: "Wild Flower" by the New Birth. It's an oldie but a goodie.

Here we were at day 211, as noted in my journal. Time flew, and I noted in the journal, "Will the journal be full before I have my book written?" Enjoying life, love, thoughts, and dreams as each page turned, I documented our times together. To me, it meant everything for us to be enjoying life, but I also wanted to finish the book so everyone could read our story. I was motivated daily, but the days flew by so fast. Life had too many demands, and time seemed so limited in a day. Every moment was a new memory—a cherished moment to hold in our hearts forever. It did my heart good to continue watching Robert become stronger and stronger.

For our anniversary in 2016, in July, we went to an outdoor BBQ at a friend's, took our Camaro to a park for a car show, and walked hand in hand. We had company, and it was just another fantastic weekend.

Robert was now seven months out since the transplant. Robert continued to adjust well to the medications and looked well. We thanked God every morning and night for this gift that he deserved.

When I look back on all the wonderful texts I received from people at the time of his surgery, I am amazed at how heartfelt and caring people can be and how much it helps you to have support.

A hundred days passed since the gift. Life continued. I daily gave thanks.

It was now day 332. Robert was approaching day 333. There was no infection and no rejection! We mailed our Gift of Life letters to the donor family today. I will share those in the next chapter when I introduce you to them. You'll see the letters we wrote, the phone calls, and the visits we shared.

Forty days passed, and we received a letter from the mother of the donor (November 26, 2016). I could tell already that she was an amazing woman.

It was December 9, 2016, and Robert was a year out from his surgery. Everything was just great at his one-year checkup! Where did the last year go? It doesn't take much for me to think back to his hospital stay and all that we went through. Every time I pull out the journal where I noted things, I am constantly reminded of the struggle, but I remember that we made it through. And a few more visits at this time to make sure all is well.

On day 348, our close friend Jamey received his call for his gift of life a couple of weeks ago. He was doing well. Thank the Lord. We continued to frequent the hospital support group meetings at Henry Ford and the University of Michigan.

Robert did some ice-skating recently. He wanted to be sure that he was strong enough to take me, as he knew that was one of the things I dreamed we'd be able to do together.

And he continued to tackle the honey to-do list!

As we pressed forward, the holidays were approaching, and so were the celebrations. It was yet another time to be grateful for life's blessings, and seeing Robert enjoy active time with family warmed my heart.

A hundred more days passed, and we were in 2017. And since we were in Michigan, Detroit, we had dark, cold, dreary, winterlike days. And we had cabin fever!

There were another fifty days of no journaling. The days trickled by with day-to-day living, working, and anxiety for warmer weather. There still never seemed to be enough time. We actually both had a little cold. For Robert, it was scary, but nothing became of it.

It had been four hundred days since Robert's transplant. Wow, think of that—four hundred days later. We continued to mentor others and give back. I shared our meeting flyers with the pulmonary group near my office, and they were very grateful to have more information to give their patients.

Today was a boring, dark, monotonous day. As glad as we were for the healthy, happy days, today was not a good day. It was one of those stupid, silly disagreement argument days over me not being able to find something in the house. Anyhow, as I always say, never go to bed angry or leave the house angry. I kissed Robert's cheek, and we said or apologies. Tomorrow was a new day.

Literally three months passed with no journal notations. And as I turned the page, I came across these two beautiful quotes:

> Hope is the thing with feathers floating through the day with hope.

> The soul that perpetually overflows with kindness will always be happy. AMEN.

April 1, 2017

We spent the whole day outside in our yard together, and it was beautiful. Just working in the yard and on the cars brought us both serenity.

An Unknown Angel's Gift

The days can get so monotonous for anyone, and you need to just make the best of each day by doing simple things that keep you focused and happy.

May 2017

We shared our first Tigers game together this month. It was a blast. The best part was walking that whole stadium and not getting tired. It rained some, but the food and drink were good. And so was just being able to go and enjoy this together. Here is a pic.

June 2017

We had quality time together. Did someone say *car show?*

Again we went to more car shows this season than we ever had. This show had car detailing, and we had travel miles to show them. We also walked together and saw every car at that show. And guess what? I did not see my husband get winded from walking hand in hand. He had no other care but to breathe in that fresh air and be thankful.

June 28, 2017

Robert and I played tennis together. Every day, when you do a little more together, you get a little stronger physically and emotionally.

August 2017

We were just loving life, the outdoors, summer, and all that could be done in a day!

It was now September 6. Just when we had smooth sailing, Robert worked too hard outdoors and injured his finger with wood from an old rake in the yard, and a pesky old woodchuck showed his face. Needless to say, Robert's finger started to look bad, and we went to the emergency room (we were there from 9:00 p.m. to 1:00 a.m.). We had a nice doctor (they tried to give us a medical assistant, but, well, you all know how I am). He was a transplant patient, and we needed a doctor. And the stories you hear while waiting and waiting. We had a crazy woman next to us couldn't reach her doctor and didn't want to take her medicine. The staff took good care of Robert. No fears. All healed up well.

September 16, 2017

Just when all was well, Robert was placing an American flag on a GTO at a car show when it broke off and went into his hand, and we were back at the emergency room. We went years with nothing after the transplant and had two injuries within ten days' time! A resident sewed him up. She seemed legit. A gunshot victim next to us played hoops for money and got robbed and shot. The stories you hear while waiting. The People in the room next to us had so many visitors while waiting. They were out for revenge. That's just a little excitement to add to the evening and story.

September 24, 2017

There was a Gift of Life event honoring donor families. We volunteered for this event and gave name badges at the tables to donor families who lost loved ones. This ceremony honored the families who lost loved ones who were organ donors. There were great speakers. It was also very disturbing, how many families lost loved ones such as babies and teenagers, but they were able to save so many lives. Thank you.

And to our surprise, there was a Jaguar event happening this day at the same venue. Of course, Robert and I would jump on an opportunity to drive some fast cars on a course. We made a short film and drove on a few tracks. It was a very exciting experience, and guess what? We were able to walk and drive—no getting winded or overly exerted from that!

Here are some car show pics! Look at the winners.

Just another winner.

Cherie S. Blackwell

A man and his goat.

Me and Robert—die-hard car buffs.

An Unknown Angel's Gift

Robert bought the second car (automatic) for us when it was getting too difficult to shift in the GTO. Months after the purchase, we got the life-saving phone call. Needless to say, it's nice to have two toys!

Best in show.

Me out for a spin in a fast Chevy.

Two guys out for a spin.

My very first trophy.

Rob and me catching a cool car show downtown
in Belleville, Michigan. #selfiesatcarshows

Just a man able to work on his car!

An Unknown Angel's Gift

This is our mad, bad Camaro—fun, fun, fun. *Vrooomm*.

Here are some other enjoyable events we shared as time went by.

Greg and Claudia's (Mom and Pop's) wedding.

Dinner with cousins Paul, Guy, their spouses and children, and my dad and stepmom.

One of the many dinners we shared with our favorite people: Bill (my brother), Joan (Bill's wife), Claudia, and Dad. This pic was taken six months before Robert's transplant, and two years later, this was the location where we would meet up with his "donor family." You will hear all about them in the next chapter.

One of the many dinners we shared with two of our favorite people: Mike (Robert's brother) and his wife, Lori.

All smiles.

Hockey is a blast, especially with Greg (my dad), me, Michael (Robert's brother), and Robert.

Cheers! Robert and I love to go out for adult beverages.

This place was the Dirty Dog Jazz Café. We had wanted to see for years, and we finally went! The sign was so appropriate! Life is Good.

An Unknown Angel's Gift

And let's not forget the house projects we started and completed. When you talk and dream about it for years and it finally happens!

Many rooms and furniture later—complete. It was lots of hard work, and we got a great result!

Friends make life better. Transplant buddies.
Robert and Jamey both with oxygen above.

Both Without oxygen here. Both Blessed with the gift of life.

An Unknown Angel's Gift

Again, friends make life so much better! Pictured here are Stephanie, Debbie, and me.

They are the flowers of life! Pictured here are Terry, me, Lori, and Dawn.

Robert and Pete at the UAW Hall.

Robert and Tom in Frankenmuth.

Summertime BBQs and the ladies of the Lunn family chilling: me, Stephanie, Joan, Claudia, and Andrea.

BBQ-ing and outdoor fun and games for the guys at my brother Bill's house. Pictured here are Bill, Ty, Greg, Scott, and Robert.

Friends for over thirty-five years: Debbie, me, Shelly, and Kim.

An Unknown Angel's Gift

Alane—my friend for over thirty years—and her sweet daughter Eve.

Lene—another great friend for over thirty years.

Me with Rebecca, a great friend for years. Pictured here also is her son Joshua and her daughter Allison.

December is family time and a time to be very thankful.

What another great year we were blessed with. As the doctors put Robert through a thorough round of tests, there was nothing extreme to report. He came out with flying colors, as always. In two years since the surgery, they only treated him for a small viral infection.

An Unknown Angel's Gift

But still, as I continue to watch Robert become stronger and stronger every day, the gift is still just as meaningful as the day he received it. Every day is filled with blessings; but in the holidays, when you spend time with family, it is even more meaningful.

Two more years passed already, and there were so many (healthy) memories created. It fills my heart with joy. The days had gone by so fast, and we are living each one to the fullest. I think 2018 went by faster than 2017; the seasons pass, and Robert stays in good health and continues to look younger and younger.

As I close out this chapter, I want to share family pictures from the holidays with the Blackwells and Lunns. Family support is everything. And making memories and sharing laughter are what make life complete.

The Blackwells.
Back row, left to right: Tim, Robert, and Michael Jr.
Front row, left to right: Collin, Jeff, and Michael Sr.

Back: Tracey.
Third row, left to right: Alyssa, Kristyn, Lori, Kaylei, and Carly.
Second row, left to right: Cherie and Wendy.
Front: Eve.

An Unknown Angel's Gift

Back: Robert, Scott, and Bill.
Middle: Cherie, Andrea, Joan, and Claudia.
Front and center: Dad.

When I think about all the adjustments and about living life, I think of all the things that make it so special. This chapter reflected on Robert coming home, recovering, and living life again.

Here are some life lessons to remember as you go through life, as said by an elderly man I read about, plus a few words I added!

- Always accept an outstretched hand and have a firm handshake or steady hug.
- Look people in the eye.
- Sing and dance in the shower.
- Own a great stereo system.
- Never give up on anyone; miracles happen every day.
- Whistle.

- Avoid too much sarcasm.
- Make it a habit to do nice things for people who will never find out.
- When playing games with children, let them win.
- Be romantic.
- Be the most positive and enthusiastic person you know.
- Loosen up, relax, and enjoy life with no regrets.
- Be a good loser.
- Be a good listener.
- Keep it simple.
- Remember, no one makes it alone. Have a grateful heart and be quick to acknowledge those who helped you.
- Take charge of your attitude. Don't let others choose it for you Wake up each day with a grateful heart and be thankful.
- Show respect to everyone.
- Become someone's hero.
- Marry for love.
- Don't expect life to always be fair.

God has truly blessed us. We know this. No day is taken for granted. Each day is a gift. Never forget this as you live your life!

An Unknown Angel's Gift

Let your light shine.

Chapter 13

God's Gift

This is your life. Do what you love, and do it often.
—Author unknown

THE YEAR 2017 WAS A year to really reflect on. It flew by extremely fast because we lived each day to the fullest thanks to Robert's donor, who cannot be thanked enough every day.

During this year, we sent our thank-you letters to Robert's donor family. Neither Robert nor I knew that each of us wrote a letter, so before we sent them, we both sat down and read each other's letters. And the tears started streaming. Both letters were very heartfelt. It was a very emotional time for us to write to the family. The very first letters were sent to Gift of Life in late 2016.

Below are the first words we sent to the donor family.

This is Robert's first letter:

> Dear donor family,
>
> My name is Robert.
> First and most important is thank you for your generosity in having your loved one donate LUNGS to me so I can live, for without this gift of life, I may not be here today.
> On December the 8th at 2015 @ approximately 9 pm, my wife and I received a call that there was a possible set of lungs available for me. We have been waiting for 8 years on the trans-

plant list. After that long, I actually gave up hope of that call ever happening.

My health was getting worse, and my breathing was at its end. I lived on oxygen 24/7 all that time.

I think of your loss every day and am saddened that your loved one passed so I could live. Bless their HEART for being an organ donor.

We have many hobbies that were put on hold for long time. We enjoyed hockey games and also have muscle cars, and NOW we are able to ENJOY them again. This year we have been to more cruises and car shows than the past years. Hockey games soon, when I feel comfortable enough to be around a lot of people who might make me ill or sick. I wear a mask all the time when in public. I am living for the TWO of us now.

And again…THANK YOU!!!!!!!

I wake up every day with a smile and thank my donor then and at bedtime for the gift I have received.

My new birthday is 12/09/2015. The day the surgery was performed. Today I am 331 days post-operation. I have had no complications or infections. So this means your loved one and I are a perfect match.

I will never forget the sacrifice your family made on our behalf, and your family will be forever in my Prayers.

THANK YOU again,
Robert

This is my thank-you letter to the donor family:

I don't know you. I don't speak of you, but I thank you every morning and night in my prayers when I thank God also for the beautiful gift that my husband, Robert, finally received.

Our phone rang at 9 p.m. on a weeknight. It was a cool evening in December, another day in our life. It was the nurse coordinator. The call we had been waiting for…for eight years…finally came. It was shock and amazement. Here it was the holiday season, and all we could believe was this is a gift from God.

To you I bet it was the most difficult decision to have to be faced with. To say goodbye to a loved one. It's tragic. It's unexpected. It's horrifying. At your holiday season, you were experiencing grief over your loss, and we were rejoicing that my husband received the gift of life he so desperately needed.

So I want to say thank you from the bottom of my heart, my whole soul. Your loved one gave my husband a new lease on life. It gave us more hope for the future. I will no longer have to watch my husband gasp for air or worry if, after exertion with any activity, he will make it.

Your difficult decision has given us the opportunity to live a more normal life again. I pray for your family every day for your strength to struggle with your loss, and I hope that one day, we can thank you face-to-face for your generosity. ♥

This is Robert's reply letter (May 2017) after receiving a letter from the donor family:

Dear Angela [donor family],

I have to start this with "THANK YOU" again for your unselfish donation to the Gift of Life and me.

I am sorry for the delay in replying to your kind thoughts and words. This is a very difficult task. I am at a loss for words to describe how emotional we get when referring to our benefit but also your loss.

We pray every morning and night, giving thanks to you and your family but mostly to your son for having been an organ donor.

I, to this day, seventeen months since my transplant, have had no rejection or infection. The Lord put this union together, and I promise your son's legacy will continue as long as I am able to make it possible.

We look forward to meeting you and learning more about your son. Also, I would like for you to listen to his lungs inside me, still sustaining life.

Again, my heartfelt thanks for your time.

Robert Blackwell and wife, Cherie

October 2, 2017

We received our second letter from the donor family. The donor's name was William. God rest his soul.

October 25, 2017

We sent the following letter, the third reply to Angela's warm letter to us (I left the punctuation on these the way we originally did them)!

> Dear Angela and family,
>
> It was with great pleasure to hear back from you. I can now put a name to my donor, and that is super. I tell people about my hero but never knew his name was William.
>
> We are looking forward to meeting you and your family for more information on your son and pictures.
>
> Our lives have changed tremendously because of your kind, caring, and unselfish son. William is in my thoughts and prayers daily.
>
> I hope to hear from you soon. You can choose a time and a place that works for you.
>
> Best wishes,
> Sincerely,
> Robert and Cherie [our cell numbers were listed on this one]

November 3, 2017

We received a call from Gift of Life, and they said they were going to send us as well as the donor family release paperwork.

December 9, 2017

Robert was two years posttransplant today, and I wanted to do something extra special. Since we are both very big hockey fans, we went to a hockey game at the new arena! We each had a Bloody Mary and cheered to being able to be out, enjoying one of our favorite things together with no oxygen and no worries!

January 13, 2018

We received a Gift of Life correspondence with a name from the donor family and their address information. Robert wanted to reach out to the family, and we hoped to meet them this year.

January 27, 2018
Saturday

Robert's donor's (William) mother (Angela) called the house today at 9:00 a.m. We both shed so many tears. It was so nice to speak to the mother of the man who saved Robert's life. We immediately thought, *What an amazing strong woman this is.* She spoke very highly of her son. She said everyone called him Two *G*s (God's gift) and Fat Daddy (she said he was a big, lean man). He was very well loved. It filled my heart with joy to know that such a person saved Robert's life. We would schedule a day in the future to meet the family.

February 2, 2018
Saturday and my birthday (fiftieth!)

Angela phoned today at 10:00 a.m. It was a forty-five-minute call. She shared more information on William. Robert shared with her that he went on social media to look her and her family up and saw a picture of William. It was truly a blessing to hear Robert talking with the mother of his donor. He was so very grateful.

February 9, 2018
Saturday

Angela phoned today with her sister Zee Zee on the line as well (three-way call). We were setting up a dinner, and it was going to be this month.

February 11, 2018

Robert stated that what gave him extra motivation to write the donor family a letter was Ron B—his story about his transplant. He never got to meet his family, but he had an adoptive one he met through the transplant games. We had been fortunate enough to have communications with the donor family and be meeting.

February 17, 2018
The Masters Restaurant
Dinner with Robert's donor family

The attendees were as follows:

- Robert and Cherie
- Greg and Claudia (Cherie's parents)
- Jeff (older brother)
- Bill (Cherie's brother) and Joan (wife)
- Jamey (friend)
- Angela (Donor's mom)
- Zee Zee (Angela's sister)
- Pam (Angela's sister) and Cleve (Angela's brother-in-law)
- Keith (Pam's son) and Kobe (Pam's grandson)
- Lisa

An Unknown Angel's Gift

They brought a beautiful orchid/peace lily plant for me and a rock for Robert with the word *breathe* engraved on it.

We met for five hours at Masters. We brought a stethoscope, and Angela listened to her son's lungs. Zee Zee even brought their mom up from Texas on an iPad so we could FaceTime with her as well.

It was a beautiful night filled with love, laughter, and tears. The food, drink, and dessert were amazing. When we sat and laughed with this family, it felt like we had known them for years. Since this meet and greet, we have had dinner numerous more times with different family members on both sides, every time more fun than the last. (The dates are approaching in the next few pages.)

We were eternally grateful to have this family in our lives. No words could ultimately thank or describe our gratefulness to their son's generosity to be an organ donor. Without him, many lives would not have been saved on that night in December. This family had a huge loss and found it in their hearts to let us be a part of their lives, and for that, we would always be grateful. This was God's work. He wanted our families to know one another to lift one another up!

As the months passed by, I could say with a huge smile that Robert and I were discussing more and more home improvements. One of my greatest hopes was that one day, we could plan and do home projects together in and outside the house. We were putting plans together, shopping together, and planning, and I loved it.

April 2018

Three weeks passed, and the house-renovation floor project was done. Robert did a *great* job. The best part of all of this was seeing him be able to do it!

April 14, 2018

On this day, we had the second donor family dinner. Today we met a brother of Angela's and one of William's sons. Two of Robert's other brothers attended today and were also with their significant others! Another good time was had by all.

May 30, 2018

The donor's mom, Angela, called us today and said some very beautiful things that were very special to us. We were so blessed.

Throughout this whole process, you talk to people along the way, and many are acquaintances you have known for many years. One day in particular, when I was out, a woman I knew inquired how Robert was doing, and I expressed how well he was doing and that we had met the donor's family. She was in tears, very touched. I said, "Robert is a poster child for transplants."

I'm not sure where this quote or saying came from, but I wrote it at this time in our lives: "Like rivers, our hearts intertwine. Two hearts are better than one."

June 23, 2018

On this day was our third dinner with the donor family. We always met at the Masters Restaurant! Today we got to meet the rest of Angela's sisters. There was one brother of hers that we had not met. We had another amazing dinner. My dad did a wonderful painting of William (aka Two *G*s / Fat Daddy) and gave it to Angela. She loved it. There was lots of sharing from all tonight. My dad mentioned how I was in the process of writing a book, and it was a very nice complimentary moment.

And then I came across this quote this evening: "Hope is a good thing—maybe the best of things."

August 2018

I mention this now in this chapter because without the generosity of Robert's donor, William, this would not have happened. We took our first vacation in ten years (out of the state). It brings tears to my eyes, just thinking about it. The fact that we did not have to pack oxygen or plan everything around the fact of timing and enough oxygen and the fact that I did not have to watch my husband, Robert, stress about that aspect of going anywhere filled my heart with joy. We traveled, and we thanked William every day. Even though it rained on our vacation, it didn't matter. I spent it with my healthy husband, and we couldn't have been happier. Thank you, William.

But then Robert had a gallbladder attack, and all our festivities were cut short. It was scary, but we came home, saw the doctors, and got it taken care of (this was on August 6, 2018). I have to mention shortly that before the procedure, we held each other close and said a prayer together. He got teary-eyed and mentioned his donor, William, aka Fat Daddy or Two *G*s. We had grateful hearts. All did go well. Better luck eating a big hearty meal early on our next vacation, Robert! We had a day with a scare: Robert got a low-grade fever. But it passed! Whenever Robert woke feeling blah, he'd snap out of it. He was so tough! Nothing germlike would get him down!

It was the day before Dream Cruise 2018—another event we were able to truly enjoy without oxygen. Thank you, donor—William! We had a blast, cruising Woodward before it was even Woodward Cruise. My husband was full of compliments. We had a great meal, and we just loved the simple times of laughter and cruising together in good health. While we were out enjoying life, I saw this bumper sticker that said "Live simply so others may simply live."

Life is full of so many blessings, and you have to enjoy the simpler things and not sweat the small stuff. You have to appreciate every moment and not let things get you down! And the day of the cruise was simply fabulous with lots of great people, great times, and ice cream! Thank you, William.

August 26, 2018

Another great time was had because Robert was well enough to live it. We enjoyed a cruise in late August (Hines). We were cruising, walking, running, talking, laughing, and driving more, which made every day complete. Thank you, William. Here is yet another quote I came across this day: "Just breathe, just live, just be you."

September 6 to 9, 2018

And yet another vacation was made possible because of Robert's donor: Frankenmuth Autofest. Our longtime friends Tom and Deb had asked us for over ten years to participate in the festivities, and we could finally do this! Being able to create more memories is what life is about. Thanks to Robert's donor, we could continue to live this life together. I tracked our steps on the pedometer and found that we walked over fifty thousand steps, people! Can I say there was an event one night where Robert looked at me on the dance floor just like he did over twenty years ago? It does a heart good when you can enjoy time with the one you love along with laughter, great people, great food, great drink, and great cars!

October 4, 2018

Robert has a big Doctor appointment with extensive tests and I won't go into details. One of his medications dosages were increased and so far so good. No rejection!

An Unknown Angel's Gift

October 20, 2018

We had another amazing dinner with the donor family. We celebrated William's (Two *G*s / Fat Daddy) birthday. It was a beautiful time had by all of us. Each time we went, we were meeting more family, and more of ours had been able to attend the dinners also.

October 2018

The chief of transplant invited us to the fiftieth anniversary transplant gala event—a black-tie event to honor transplant physicians and patients. Robert took me shopping for a dress. It was pretty exciting!

When I started this book, little did I know that I would be writing a chapter about my husband's (Robert) donor family. We have been truly blessed. Being able to meet the hero's family was beyond words. We were so grateful to have this family in our lives.

November 2, 2018

Tonight marked the Henry Ford gala event. Robert and I dressed up in formal attire (Robert looked incredible in his tux, and I got my hair done along with some jewelry and shoes). It was an absolute honor for us to be invited to such an incredible event honoring so many doctors, staff, and patients. We ran into so many old faces and new faces. The food, drinks, and conversation were invigorating. The decorations were incredible. It was held at the MGM in Detroit. We danced the night away. Thank you, Henry Ford. Thank you, donor. Every time I am able to dance with my husband or we are able to enjoy an activity, I thank you, William, for being a donor. You gave us our lives back.

November 3, 2018

Today held another exciting event. It was our nephew Collin and his beautiful bride Wendy's wedding day. It was an exceptional wedding and reception. And we were dressed up once again! The location was beautiful. It was so nice to spend time with the Blackwell family and meet the rest of Wendy's family. I was able to attend her bridal shower earlier in the year. We took lots of pictures and once again danced the night away. We even spent time with the wedding party (after-party!) afterward for hours. It was a great, great weekend. Thank you, donor.

The holidays passed so quickly. There was another Henry Ford transplant holiday party with so many heartwarming stories of patients doing well. There were family gatherings on my side and Robert's—again, more times we could enjoy thanks to Robert being able to breathe and get around without becoming exerted. We rang in the new year. We made it through the winter. Robert was able to snow-blow again (with extreme excitement), and we celebrated my birthday. There were more and more things he was able to do because of his donor, William.

March 30, 2019

We had a wonderful dinner with the donor family this afternoon. We met William's two brothers today and were so glad we did. Every time we went to dinner, we had such an appreciation for this family and the love and respect they showed one another. My heart was filled with joy to know they were going to be in our lives forever. Again, thank you, donor—William.

April through June 2019

Where had the days gone? We had done lots around house and lots with the cars. I continued to see Robert doing more and more around the house and with the cars. His enthusiasm, determination, and drive had always been incredible, even with the oxygen slowing him down; however, since the transplant, every day he looked younger and became stronger. I have said it before and I will say it again: every time I saw him able to do things, it made my day every day. He struggled for so long. We struggled for so long. I prayed every day for our prayers to be answered. They were. Each day was a gift. Thank you, donor—William.

July 7, 2019

We were invited to a donor family function (graduation party)! We looked forward to meeting more and more of William's family. Today was an absolutely amazing day. Seeing this wonderful family interacting and meeting so many more of them was inspirational. We felt so blessed to have them in our lives.

Here is a passage that Williams Aunt Zee Zee wrote:

Good Afternoon Facebook Family and Friends,

Let me put a story behind the (2) pictures that are posted. 2GG's was an Organ Donor, he saved (4) lives. This gentleman here that is pictured below was the young man that received both of FatDaddy's Lungs he is the gentleman that is wearing the blue t-shirt in the picture on the left (our first meeting). During our 1st meeting he told us that he wanted to meet us 6 months after the surgery but, he was informed to wait, he explained how things was going thru his head like the fear of meeting us and if we wanted to meet with him.

In this walk of life, I have learned that WE as the People can not handle GOD's business. For example: We can not make man from our OWN Dirt. God places PEOPLE in your LIFE for a reason and sometimes we never know what that reason is. This gentleman was placed in our lives because he received 2GG's Lungs and that was a BLESSING FROM GOD, he had been waiting for 8 years and 8 in the BIBLE is a NEW BEGINNING. God knows that we the MANLEY's are a LOVING FAMILY and that WE ARE A SILLY FAMILY (LOL). But, meeting this FAMILY just made it one BIG SILLY AQUARIUM OF MEETING a family just as SILLY as WE ARE. Both sides were WELCOMED with OPEN ARMS. I THANK GOD EVERYDAY FOR MY NEW NEPHEW (NIECE) AND HIS FAMILY, I THANK GOD FOR THE JOY WITH MY PAIN AND MOST OF ALL I THANK GOD FOR YOU!

#2GG'sYOULIVEONTHRUROBERT

To those of you who are recipients, here are the guidelines Gift of Life uses to write your donor family:

> Writing to Your Donor Family
> Guidelines for Transplant Recipient
>
> The decision to write to your donor family is a very personal one. Donor families consistently express gratitude about hearing from their loved one's recipients and appreciate the communication. There is no time limit to write to your donor family. We suggest that you write to your donor family when you are healthy and feel comfort-

able. Writing to your donor family can be as simple as signing a "Thank You" card or "Thinking of You" card. All correspondence is anonymous, and Gift of Life Michigan respects the privacy of our recipients and donor families.

Things you can include:
a thank-you card with the letter

- Write about yourself, family, hobbies, interests, etc.
- Write about your personal transplant experience, how it has affected your life.
- Acknowledge the donor family's loss and express gratitude for your gift of life.
- Note: Sign only your first name. Please do not include specific information about yourself (i.e., last name, address, city, telephone number or email address, name of employer, etc.).

Here is a wide array of pics of William (the donor), his family, and some of the many events I mentioned in this chapter that we were able to attend because of William. We honor him every day because without him, this life would not have been possible. This has been quite the journey, and we create more and more memories every day and cherish each day with each breath. And with each thank-you, we move forward, enjoying life. Like I said, we share a lot of stories and laughter when we are together, and we are forever grateful for this family God put into our lives.

William McGee (October 22, 1982–December 8, 2015). May God rest his soul.
This is the man who saved Robert Blackwell's life!
Two lungs. (Two *G*s / Fat Daddy).

An Unknown Angel's Gift

Here is the picture my father painted of William for the family.

The artist Greg Lunn.

Robert with his donor's mother, Angie (what a beautiful woman inside and out).

Robert with William's uncle Cleve.

An Unknown Angel's Gift

Angie and me.

Cherie, Angie, and Robert.

Robert, Cherie Pam and Angie

Cherie S. Blackwell

Angie (donor mom) and Robert (recipient).

There are nothing but smiles in all the pictures. How do you put into words and thank the family whose family member saved your spouse's life? There are not enough words to express my heartfelt gratitude.

Here we are with Angie at another summer event with the donor family.

An Unknown Angel's Gift

August 2019

We recently took another vacation in August 2019. We took a picture of William (Two *G*s [God's gift]) with us. As the wind blew through the trees of all the state parks we visited, I thanked God as I watched my husband, Robert, walk the trails up and down the mountains, swim in the ocean, and thoroughly enjoy a meal, a drink, a laugh, and a moment. It's another memory we can make because of this man's selfless gift to be an organ donor. He made all of our todays possible and all our hopes, dreams, and future memories to cherish possible.

We attended numerous car events and were able to create many memories with friends and family.

I could not even count how many times I became choked up from just thinking about what a gift/blessing we were given.

I would like to share some words I wrote to share at the first donor family dinner gathering (I did not share them as my father gave a fantastic toast, which I felt was so incredible). Here are my words:

> There are not enough words to thank your son for his generosity. Every day, I have prayed for your family's strength in your loss and thanked God for giving Robert and me a new lease on life; to not have to watch him struggle to breathe every day is a blessing. Every day is a gift. We take nothing for granted. It is an honor to meet you and thank you face-to-face. I want to thank everyone here for their support. And to the ones who cannot be here, thank you. Thank you for your huge support.

There is always a moment in each day where I stop and thank God for his many blessings.

I would like to close this chapter with a picture of William and Robert.

An Unknown Angel's Gift

An Unknown Angel's Gift

An Unknown Angel's Gift

Cherie S. Blackwell

Here's a quote from the prospect church service with the donor family: "When it is a questions of God's almighty spirit, never say, 'I can't.'"

Chapter 14

Organ Donation Education— Myths and Facts

Faith is the substance of things hoped for.
—Unknown author

IN THIS CHAPTER, I WILL discuss organ donation myths and facts as well as morale and how to build your current relationships—things I have learned throughout this whole process.

Throughout the years, Robert and I have been to over ten years of transplant support meetings and are active mentors to people coming in newly listed. We feel it is important to give back. We also are volunteers for Gift of Life Michigan. By educating others of the importance of organ donation, you give back. We try to wear Donate Life pins or clothing often, tell Robert's story, work tables at events, and volunteer at events to educate others. And by attending these events, we also hear a new organ donation story that touches our hearts. People are always shocked to hear how long Robert waited for his lungs, but he is a proven success; he's a poster child for lung transplantation. And just giving hope to others is so important. Many schools and colleges have their students hearing lectures about organ donation and realizing the importance of how one organ donor can save and enlighten so many lives. We come across many skeptical people, and after we tell our story, they want to become organ donors! That is pretty awesome!

Cherie S. Blackwell

As you read in the first chapter of this book, it is so frightening no matter what age you are to have a debilitating disease and not be able to work or live your daily lifestyle as you wish you could. As a newly married young adult, you never expect to be told you're sick and be informed of all the adjustments you have to make. In this process of meeting people and all that we have been through, we realized that it is so important to educate people and give them hope that they will get that call someday. We have met so many different people from different walks of life, and it is amazing to see them be in the pretransplant process—them being listed and having fears and questions—and then get their transplant. And they have obstacles, but they get through those also. For us, continuing to give back and support those coming in fresh is very important to us. We were in their shoes and know how fearful it is—the questions, the doubts, the myths, the facts, the support that you need desperately from people at the hospital, your family and friends, and the lessons you learn and teach along the way.

Every state has an organ procurement organization where they try to match donors with recipients. Depending on where the organ comes from, the organ procurement organization (OPO) from that state will work with the process.

For those of you questioning organ donation, I want you to think about if you had a loved one slowly deteriorating and losing hope. Wouldn't you want to do everything in your power as well as hope and pray that someone could help them live a better life? There are a lot of ungrateful, self-centered, hateful, angry, unhappy people in this world. When I come into contact with people like this, I just smile and always say hello or good morning or ask, "How are you?" Sometimes people just need that. They may be miserable in this life, but if there is one thing, a very important thing—a very important lesson—I have learned, it is that everyone is fighting their own battle, so just be kind and pray for them. Everyone handles things in their lives differently, and you have to have compassion and understanding. If you are going through such a situation (as I have discussed in this whole book), I would give the advice "Make sure you have communication." You have to really listen to what the other person is saying. Pay attention. What is it that they need? Maybe they need to be alone, maybe they need a

An Unknown Angel's Gift

hug, or maybe they just need you to listen, really listen. In meeting all the many spouses over the years, I have seen just how difficult of an acceptance process it is for them. It will work if you make it work. It's marriage; it is for better or worse. Some people can't do it. But can I just offer up some advice? Think of all the things you love about this person, and as yourself if they would be as supportive of you if the shoe was on the other foot. I wasn't going anywhere. Every day, I awoke with hope and positivity and still do because it takes work and strength. Do you have what it takes?

I would like to share the speech I shared at a lung transplant support meeting exactly one year after Robert had his transplant.

> This time last year, during the holidays, we spent it in the ICU. After waiting eight years for that call, we have been so blessed. The call finally came—one we had been waiting for. Robert has been very lucky to have no infection, rejection, or hospitalization. We are thankful for our wonderful family and friends and the staff here. [I am quite sure I have said this numerous times in the book.] However, I thank God and the donor family for this new lease on life for my husband/us. We have our lives back. We enjoyed our muscle cars all summer and outdoor activities, and I watched my husband do things without struggling to catch his breath! We continue to go to support meetings. To hear Robert breathe so well makes my every day complete. I am just so grateful. We are looking forward to hockey games, skating, and vacations. Thank you, God bless you, and Merry Christmas.

Taking some steps back, I would like to share a card I gave Robert in 2010 (he had been listed for two years at this point):

> I love the little things you do. I wonder if you know how much I appreciate you. Thank you for the way you reach out to hold my hand, the way you cuddle me, the way you make me laugh with just a look, the way you pick me up when I am feeling down, and the way you share things I enjoy. Today I just want to let you know how much I appreciate the little things and thank you for loving me in all the special ways you do.

That same year, I received a card from Robert:

> Until now, until you, there were places in my heart I'd never been before, moments in the day I'd never appreciated before, promises in the night I'd never dreamt before until now, until you.

Both are very nice cards. In spite of all we were going through and two years into the process, we still appreciated each other. Couples need to appreciate one another and not just in the difficult times. Of course, it is the most difficult thing to go through an illness with your spouse; some days you will question if you will survive it, but you will draw strength somehow and make it!

What is the biggest lesson learned throughout this whole process? I think it is that we are all human and can all learn more patience and understanding, and I learned by watching someone struggle and be stronger than anyone I have every met (and I am not just saying that!) that all things are possible—that life only gives you as much as you can handle. Do I look back and wonder how we made it? Of course, but you learn building blocks and apply everything you have learned.

I still look back and wonder how we made it with so many obstacles, doctors, fears, and hopes; but as I said, I watched a very strong person never complain.

Here is another piece of advice: don't sweat the small stuff. Have an outlet with friends or family or a hobby, and make sure you do it.

You need that time to decompress, gather your thoughts, and maintain your sanity. This was another big lesson I learned.

Another valuable piece of advice is this: let your family and friends be supportive. It is a learning process for everyone!

Caregivers

Utilize your FMLA with work. The doctors and staff are happy to complete the necessary paperwork you get from your employer to turn in. It helps in the long run.

A couple of suggestions from a meeting attendee many years ago was for women patients: wear a sports bra and a tee to make testing easier.

Here are some things Robert and I learned: Take water bottles to restaurants (you do not know their process for buckets of ice, and those bins can be very dirty. And if that bucket hits the floor and is stacked in another with ice, you're getting that next glass of water with that dirty ice). Take plastic utensils in the first year to restaurants. Avoid buffets.

Here is the resource guide that was given to us at the day of discharge after transplant:

> *Appointments.* Attend weekly clinic appointments for the first four weeks, then biweekly if the patient is doing well. These weekly appointments consist of labs, chest x-rays, spirometry pulmonary function testing, and clinic with a doctor.
> The doctor may want a bronchoscopy test in a month's time.
> If there are heart issues, which can arise with some patients (Robert had gotten A-fib after his transplant), you will have echoes (heart ultrasounds) four to six weeks after transplant to evaluate the heart.
> You must make an appointment with your primary care physician within one week of being discharged.

Medications. What you need to know are the following:

- names (both)
- appearance and purpose of the medication

Schedule and dosage. Take them at the same time every day: 9:00 a.m. and 9:00 p.m.
Refill them with plenty of time to spare. You cannot go without these immunosuppressant drugs, and it is very important to be compliant so you stay as well as possible.
Use your blue book daily.
Common side effects.
On the day of your discharge, be ready! Have your support system take notes and be helpful. It is a very stressful yet exciting time, and there is a lot to remember!
Some other items to remember at discharge. Your labs must be done between 8:00 a.m. and 10:00 a.m. before your Prograf dose, and your results will be given to you via a call within one to three days. This is important. As they review your labs, they will adjust your dosages accordingly for some time until your levels are where they should be. They will have standing orders in the system so you can have your labs done at a Henry Ford facility closer to your home.
Diet You should eat seated in an upright position and remain upright for one to two hours.
As an FYI, they may give you a list of other foods to avoid if you're on certain medications!
Foods to avoid include the following: raw or rare meat, fish, and uncooked or undercooked eggs—

no dipper eggs! Eat meat well-done. Avoid salad bars and deli counters. Buy vacuum-packed lunch meats only instead of freshly sliced. *No* grapefruit. Regarding dairy, only drink pasteurized milk, yogurt, cheese, and other dairy products. Avoid soft, mold-ripened, blue-veined cheeses such as Brie, Camembert, Roquefort, Stilton, Gorgonzola, and blue cheese.

As for water, avoid well water. Boil it for one minute before drinking, if you must. Drink bottled water.

Things to report to your nurse coordinator:

- increase in temperature from baseline to one degree
- any swelling
- increased pain
- redness or cough
- sputum production
- decreased spiro results by 10 percent
- If the patient has a fever over 100.5 degrees, go to the ER and page your coordinator.

One thing Robert had to do in the hospital was have breathing treatments of AmBisome (which tasted awful, as per Robert).

This will be thoroughly explained by the nurses for you to do at home (you will have already done them at the hospital).

A Prednisone burst will sometimes be dispensed. You will be notified of this if this is the case at discharge.

Dental antibiotics. These are very important; they must be taken prior to any dental procedure/cleaning.

Now here is an example of our schedule after Robert was discharge and came home:

January 2016:

- First week: visiting nurse (twice) and physical therapist (once)
- Second week: visiting nurse (twice) and physical therapist (thrice) (breathing treatments done); a visit to the doctor for labs, x-rays, and blows; a surgeon visit; and medications called in for changes
- Third week: visiting nurse (once) and physical therapist (thrice), a visit to the medical doctor, run errands (e.g., to have food in house), a clinic visit
- Fourth week: a clinic visit, visiting nurse (once) and physical therapist (twice), labs, and kidney doctor visit (they watch your kidneys closely as medications tend to be harsh on them)

In between all these visits, you'll be scheduling follow-ups after these appointments for your medical doctor (who will check your INR level if you were placed on Coumadin; this must be monitored closely). You will need to schedule all follow-up doctor appointments in a timely manner.

The subsequent months to follow—months 2 (which will be as month 1 [for us, it was anyway], 3, 4, 5, and 6—all involve close monitoring and numerous appointments. Keep a hard calendar to keep track of all your items.

I suggest keeping a binder with sections for insurance-related billing matters, documents of who you talk to and the dates, and all doctor visits as you will see many different ones (possibly). Keep a log of the different offices' phone numbers. Maybe that is just me, but it helps to be organized, because it can all seem so overwhelming at first. But I found it helpful to have the calendar in front of me, and I wrote down notes during and after visits of what was needed for the follow-ups.

As you go through this process, you will enhance and build relationships along the way, and you will see just how helpful and understanding people can be. A piece of advice a nurse practitioner once gave us was "*If* equals call." Never feel like you are a burden to

An Unknown Angel's Gift

the staff who are taking care of you at the hospital. They are experts in the area, and they will be able to give you the answers you need and help you understand why something is the way it is. Or they can assist you if you need to come in.

I would like to share some quotes that I can really appreciate struggling through the whole process:

> We are all moving shadows, and all our busy rushing ends in nothing. (Psalm 39:6)

> All we have to decide is what to do with the time that is given us. (J.R Tolkien)

> When you are in a season of challenge, brokenness, and failure, identify the voices that will speak not only to your current situation, we all need accountability, but to your future self.

> Find people who speak life into where you're going. (Ben Franklin, "Lost Time is Never Found Again")

An Unknown Angel's Gift

When I look back on this whole journey and what I have written I hope it will enhance others' lives and offer hope, inspiration, and a notion that transplantation works. Organ donation saves lives.

Go confidently in the direction of your dreams; live the life you have imagined. It will all work out!

Positive vibes, positive life!

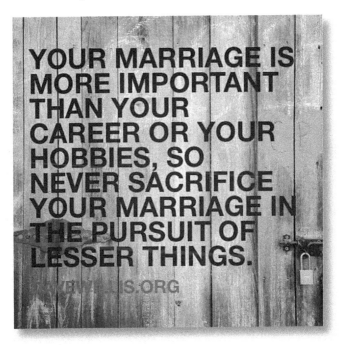

Cherie S. Blackwell

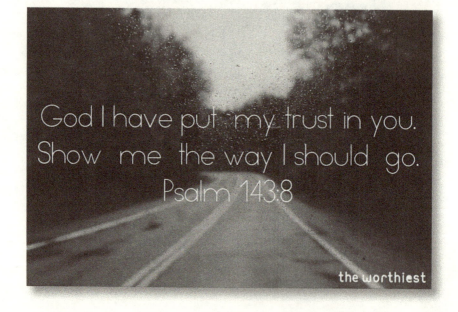

Chapter 15

Final Chapter

Strength, courage, wisdom.
—Author unknown

As I sit here, I cannot believe it is time to close/end this book. What a journey it has been for Robert, me, and our families, the eight years of waiting and all the obstacles in between! Thinking about the living of our lives in the last three-plus years, the time it has taken me to write this as I relive each moment, and even until this day, when we mentor people or talk to strangers, I am amazed at just how much I have grown and the knowledge that I have gained and can pass on to others. It amazes me how God's timing is in place in so many situations.

I was at a doctor's office, and there was a gentleman who came in (on oxygen). He sounded so defeated with his disease as he talked to the front office staff. He was turning in FMLA paperwork. As he turned to leave the office, I opened up and told him about how I could sympathize with his situation, about Robert, and about our journey. I knew in that moment that I gave that man hope. Isn't that what life should be about—giving love and hope to others, reaching out and lending a helping hand, being unselfish and giving, and being that glimmer people need to get through a situation? I can't tell you how good it felt that day after I talked to that man with such confidence and boosted his spirits. I could tell his pride had gotten the best of him, and he talked about himself and his wife and their trying to get by day to day. I sympathized, and I even inquired where he received his care and recommended Henry Ford hospital. I also said that he could always go for a second opinion. He had the defeated/giving-up attitude at the start of our conversation, but at the conclusion, he looked and acted hopeful and was smiling. I hope I helped him have a better day and think about the fact that there is hope and that there can be answers to our concerns and prayers.

There are so many influences throughout this process that I mentioned earlier in the book. These can be people in your family, friends, or people you meet through the support meetings. I remember us being new to the meetings and seeing the people who had their transplants and how they offered hope to those of us who were scared and new to the whole process, trying to accept all the changes we were forced to face. It is not easy for anyone. And when all is said and done, you are just praying your loved one's body doesn't reject the organ, and you have to go through the processes all over again!

I just want to mention some words to a few songs I thought were pretty cool. It amazes me how these artists are such great songwriters and capture such wonderful thoughts.

Here are some words to the song "Breathe" by Faith Hill (emphasis added):

> It's simple, it's beautiful, it's love! [my words]
> I can feel the magic floating in the air
> Being with you gets me that way
> I watch the sunlight dance across your face and I've
> Never been this swept away
>
> All my thoughts just seem to settle on the breeze
>   [this is me on a daily basis]
> When I'm lying wrapped up in your arms
> The whole world just fades away
> The only thing I hear
> Is the beating of your heart [this makes me think
>   of when I would put my head on Rob's chest
>   after surgery and listen to his lungs and his
>   heartbeat]

An Unknown Angel's Gift

'Cause I can feel you breathe
It's washing over me
Suddenly I am melting into you
There's nothing left to prove
Baby, all we need is to just be
Caught up in the touch
The slow and steady rush
Baby, isn't that the way that love's supposed to be
I can feel you breathe
Just breathe

In a way my heart is waking up
As the walls come tumbling down
I'm closer than I've ever felt before
And I know
And you know
There's no need for words right now [this was so us in the ICU at the hospital]

Cause I can feel you breathe
It's washing over me
Suddenly I'm melting into you
There's nothing left to prove
Baby, all we need is to just be
Caught up in the touch
The slow and steady rush
Baby, isn't that the way love is supposed to be
I can feel you breathe,
Just breathe

Here is another: "I'm Alive" by Kenny Chesney, featuring Dave Matthews (emphasis added):

So damn easy to say that life's so hard
Everybody's got their share of battle scars

Cherie S. Blackwell

As for me, I'd like to thank my lucky stars
That I'm alive and well

It'd be easy to add up all the pain
And all the dreams you sat and watched go up
    in flames
Dwell on the wreckage as it smolders in the rain
But not for me, I'm alive

And today you know that's good enough for me
Breathing in and out's a blessing, can't you see?
Today's the first day of the rest of my life
And I'm alive and well
Yeah, I'm alive and well

Stars are dancing on the water here tonight
It's good for the soul when there's not a soul in
    sight
This boat has caught its wind and brought me
    back to life
Now I'm alive and well

And today you know that's good enough for me
Breathing in and out's a blessing, can't you see?
Today's the first day of the rest of my life
Now I'm alive and well
I'm alive and well

An Unknown Angel's Gift

I just want to say that it helps to have those bags packed and ready for when they call to let you know. A phrase I will never forget is this: "We have lungs for you, can you be here?" I remember Robert and me looking at each other, shocked. It had been so long, but we were ready (even though I took the wrong season bag)! Robert got us there safely, and the rest of the journey so far is in this book.

I truly hope you enjoyed and gained something from it, as we gained so much in this journey of anticipation, gratefulness, and life lessons. When you have your bags packed, I suggest having a little note at a place you view often. Have this note say, "Stay positive." You got this. And don't forget your phone charger, medications, the snacks you like, and a cross if you are religious. As I held Robert's parents' rosaries in my hand all night while he was under the knife, I could not sleep. I would not rest until I saw his face come out of that operating room into recovery, doing well—alive and well.

I also want to say that there was something a posttransplant recipient said at one of the recent meetings that really sums it up. She said, "Enjoy each day. Maintain the positivity. Live your best life ever"!

I have some last words before I share some pictures of laughter and love: Everyone, you don't know when your last day on this earth is. Donate life. Give the gift to someone who is waiting for a second chance. You give the recipient their life back! Organ donors are heroes.

I would like to share pics of Robert's brothers and sister and some of his nieces and nephews.

Jeff (oldest brother) and Robert.

Robert's sister Jill and her husband, Kirk.

My brother-in-law Mike, and Robert

Robert and youngest brother. Tim.

Blackwell family gathering in 2018.

An Unknown Angel's Gift

Robert and me at the Henry Ford gala to honor transplant doctors and staff, donors, and recipients.

And now we are going to ride off into the sunset in our classic cars.

Cherie S. Blackwell

    Here's to living life to the fullest and making memories to last a lifetime.
    William, thank you for saving Robert's life.

About the Author

CHERIE SUE BLACKWELL WAS BORN and raised in Detroit, Michigan, and she lived in the different suburbs of Michigan with her father and brother. She was raised around her grandparents and cousins and gained much insight from them throughout the many travels to their hometowns throughout her life. She has always loved writing poetry and reading nonfictional biographies.

She is passionate about family, friends, gardening, fashion, sports, movies, music, and the beach.

She is recognized as a mentor and volunteer for the monthly transplant support meetings as well as a Gift of Life volunteer. She has built a career with the same company for half of her life. She resides in Michigan with her husband and her cat.